Battersea Power Station

The Architectural Rebirth
of a Romantic Ruin

WilkinsonEyre

ORO
EDITIONS

Foreword and Introduction	1
1. History	7
1935–1983: A Super Power Station for the Golden Age of Electricity	10
1983–2011: A Derelict Enigma	16
Unrealised Designs, In Popular Culture	20
2. How do you solve a problem like Battersea Power Station?	22
A Modern Ruin	23
Retaining the Magic	30
The Masterplan	32
A Town within a Building	34
3. Learning the Building	37
Cataloguing the Existing	42
Restoration Strategy	46
A Huge Challenge: Navigating Scale	48
4. A Town in a Building	51
Retail	53
Events	77
Residential	83
Offices	105
Lift 109	113
Public Realm	121
5. Unlocking Challenges	130
Brickwork Matching	132
Prefabricated Brickwork	134
Control Room A	138
Control Room B	140
The Chimneys	142
Gardens in the Sky	146
Peregrine Falcon	150
Tree Structure	152
Mega Project: Logistic Endeavours	154
6. Drawings	159
7. Building Legacy	171
8. Acknowledgements	175

View from North Park

Foreword by Jim Eyre

There was a time when architects would view reworking another architect's building as a step down from designing completely new buildings, but no longer. We know we enjoy the presence of older buildings in our lives, they give a sense of the longevity of our culture and history and are a critical part of our identity. In architecture we are programmed to always respond to constraints, and a structure of Battersea Power Station's stature and scale, in its raw state, presented extraordinary opportunities that no new building would equal in quite the same way. At WilkinsonEyre, we have form in reworking industrial buildings, whether at the Hennebique concrete goods building which became 'Explore' at Bristol or the great steel mills at Rotherham transformed into 'Magna'. However, faced with the partially ruined Power Station, we already had the benefit of reviving another Giles Gilbert Scott building at Oxford University's New Bodleian Library (now the Weston Library) equipping us with an empathy to his approach to design to take forward what would become an extraordinarily complex challenge of bringing Battersea Power Station back to a new life. My own role in the venture focussed on the exciting early stages working closely with fellow director Sebastien Ricard (who led the project all the way through to completion) where we were generating ideas and evolving our own approach, sometimes tempering our natural tendencies to seek to innovate by recognising a need to preserve the essential grandeur of the building.

We felt this needed some adjustment to the way we might think about introducing new elements into a historic structure. Often there is a sound approach where the new sits in contrast to the old and the juxtaposition is enjoyable, but here the adaptations needed to be more subtle and sympathetic to the existing and sometimes in sharp contrast.

Where restoration occurs it is where the existing fabric needed repair, but also to preserve the essential spatial and aesthetic quality for instance of the Turbine Halls and Control rooms. Whereas the new residential accommodation over the switch houses and boiler house present a simple clean and unfussy appearance to the outside world, they are more inwardly articulated and domestic in scale and character with their adjoining gardens evoking a typical Georgian London square, save for the massive chimney holding each corner.

This book tells our story or moreover is a love letter to the building and records much of the work which lasted over the years from 2012 through design and construction, dominating the lives of the many who worked on it.

Introduction by Sebastien Ricard

Battersea Power Station is the ultimate example of industrial building in the twentieth century: a modern cathedral.

The aspiration of the London Power Company to make this building special was demonstrated at the outset in the commissioning of Sir Giles Gilbert Scott - at the time the most famous architect in the UK - to compose its external envelope. What followed was a busy life as an active power station, at one time producing up to a fifth of the capital's electricity. Its looming silhouette with smoking chimneys became emblematic of the industrial Thames.

After its closure in the 1980s, the building came to represent Britain's post-industrial period, and it was during this time that it was cemented in Londoners' hearts. It was at the centre of several fantasist projects. Incredible events took place there, incorporating much festivity with light shows projected onto what was rapidly becoming a young modern ruin. This came to be through a lack of maintenance, along with a succession of flawed development schemes, each taking away part of the existing fabric.

In 2012, when most felt it might be too late to restore what was now a Grade II* listed building, a Malaysian consortium decided to buy the site and redevelop the entire 42 acres. Whilst hindsight tells a different story, this was a high-risk challenge, proudly and bravely taken on by a Malaysian team, at a time when no European or North American developers wanted to touch it.

WilkinsonEyre was lucky enough to be approached to enter a competition to find a new use for the building.

I remember visiting for the first time and being driven both around and inside the building, since the site was so vast. What struck me straight away, amid this romantic industrial ruin, was the sense of scale, the incredible volumes and, of course, wherever you were in the building, the omnipresence of brick.

How does an architect tackle a challenge like Battersea Power Station when given only a three-week competition programme to come up with a design proposal?
A full design proposal would have been naive and pretentious. We could only suggest an approach by tackling fundamental questions: How could we integrate new components within the existing volume? How could we retain the sense of scale, the industrial heritage and the ageing materials which make the building so iconic? We also had to address the challenges and opportunities: How would we create smaller 'human scale spaces' in a vast set of turbine halls designed for housing major machinery and switch grids? Could we carve out voids within some of the volumes to reduce their length and width? Could we bring architectural components to break the linearity of the main volumes?

The building presented so many opportunities to explore. Beyond the exquisite detailing of the internal walls of the turbine halls – which were the perfect backdrop for any public facing activities – this vast building had multiple roofs at multiple levels. Could they be inhabited and transformed into amenities or garden for users? And the disused chimneys with their majestic verticality in the London skyline: could they be used to allow Londoners to explore their city from the sky?

It was with a set of optimistic proposals for intervention, along with freehand sketches describing our design intent, that we engaged with Battersea Power Station Development Company and their Malaysian shareholders.

The most significant pivot during that process was the recognition that, to succeed, it was imperative that the project secured long-term financial sustainability. We developed our proposals accordingly and, in conjunction with the client, created a mix of activities at scale to create what is effectively a mini city under one roof.

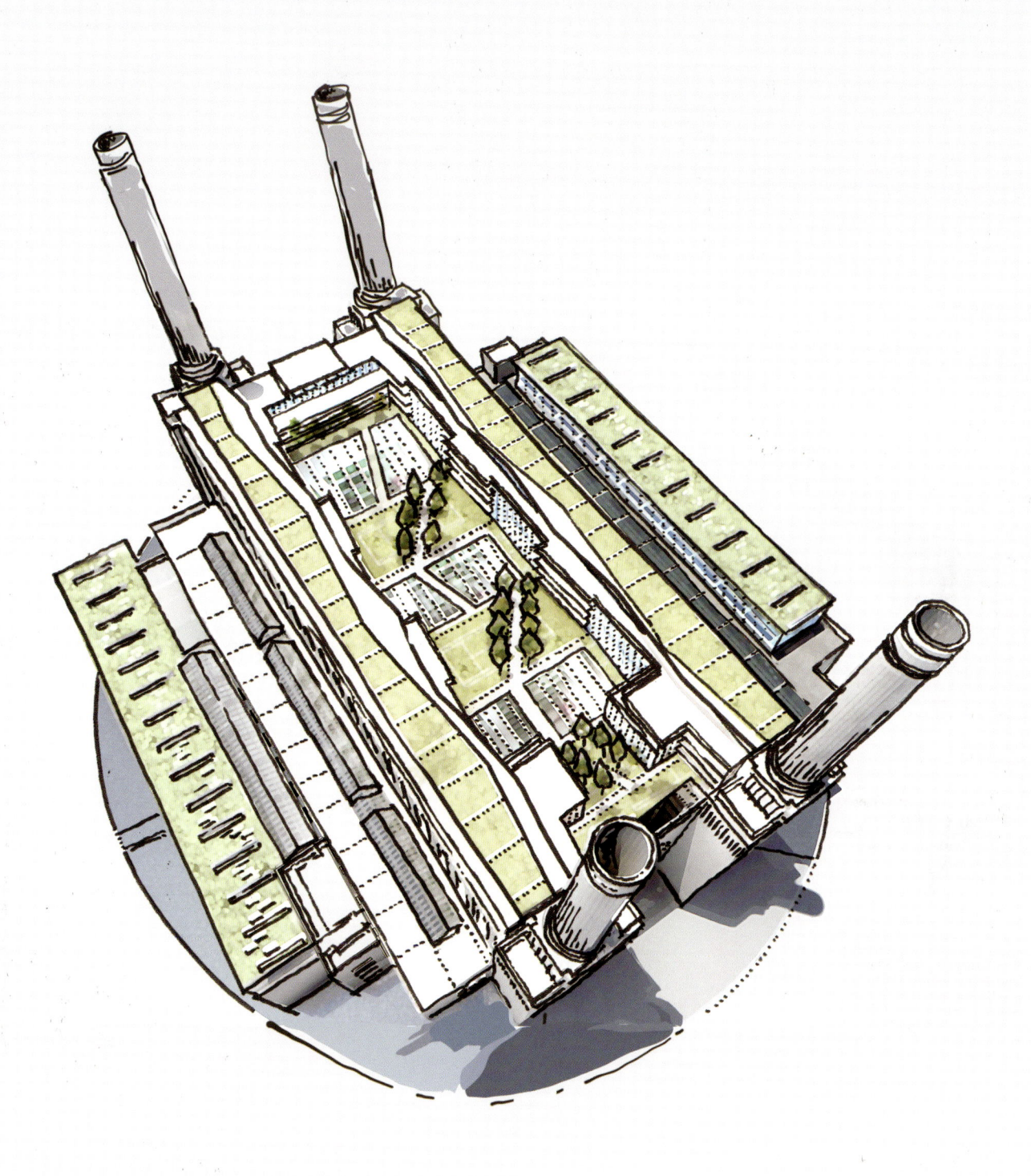

Early concept sketch exploring potential for roof landscape

Viiew from
Malaysia Square bridge

'The new interventions are sympathetic with carefully chosen palettes of materials, textures and colours. Where possible, we have allowed the original fabric of the building to tell its own story.'

What members of the public experience when wandering around the retail environment at the Power Station, or visiting the cinema, the food hall or the event space is still only a fraction of the overall building. Above these spaces are 254 residential units across the Power Station's Switch Houses and on top of the Boiler House, 45,000 sqm of offices (the size of the Gherkin), almost entirely occupied by Apple's European Campus, along with Control Room A and its ceremonial 'Director's Entrance'. At basement level, the building is once again home to an energy centre, providing and distributing energy and servicing to the overall masterplan: a huge project by any measure.

Before embarking on the major construction challenge, which at one point saw 18 cranes on site, we needed to convince the relevant heritage bodies that securing the long term future of the building required major interventions within the existing building fabric. To enable new uses required 120 new window slots, 3 storeys of new volume above the existing Switch Houses and the main Boiler House volume — all of this within a Grade II* Listed building.

The condition of some elements had deteriorated to the extent that they were dangerous structures and we had to fully evaluate whether it was feasible to retain them even with substantial repair. Justification had to be prepared for major interventions like the reconstruction of the chimneys and the open surgery on the elevations where the steel framing could only be reached and treated through opening up the brickwork. This all happened in a context of scepticism and regular campaign against the project from bodies who criticised the proposed mix of activities and would not accept that the historic fabric would need to be transformed to accommodate them.

Working on a project of this scale and complexity has been an incredible human adventure which has required dedication, abnegation and determination from all parties involved, starting with a client who was committed and convinced that the project could be an amazing new quarter in central London. This was a vision that very few believed in at the time. But Battersea Power Station Development Company (BPSDC) and their shareholders (consortium of Malaysian investors comprising PNB, Sime Darby Property, S P Setia and the Employees' Provident Fund) had the foresight to imagine Battersea being redesignated 'Zone 1' on the tube map, to invest in the creation of a new tube stop on site and have the ability to draw office tenants needing more than 400,000 sqft of space to south-west London.

Now, for the first time in its history, the building is open to the public and people can enjoy its amazing internal architectural features. Perhaps more significantly, people are colonising the building, its surrounding public realm, taking over and talking about the building.

What the project has enabled is the transformation of a building which was already iconic in terms of its architecture, silhouette and urban presence in London to a building which is now also 'owned' by the people, by Londoners and visitors, and gives to the community.

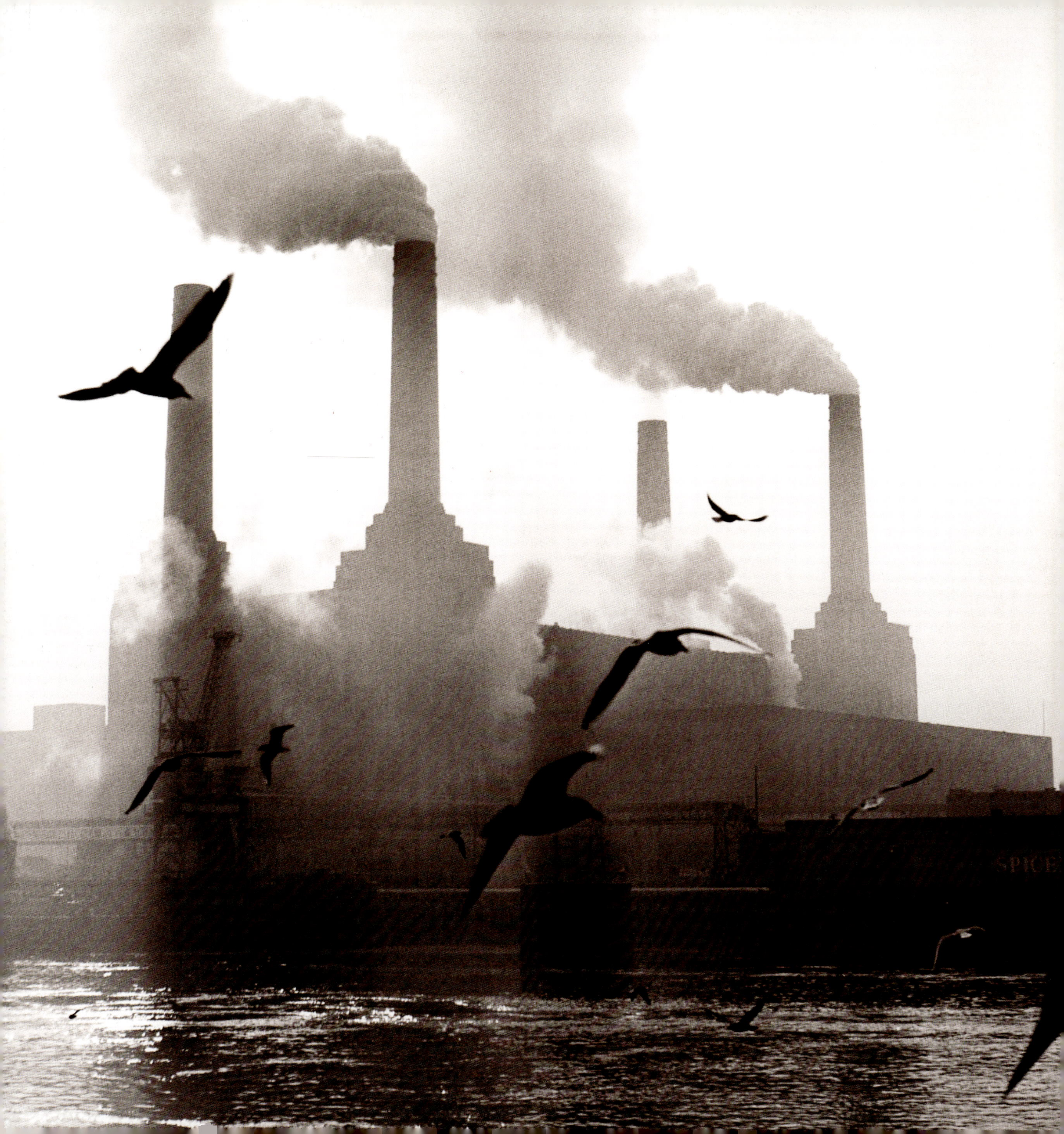

History

The Making of an Icon

1

1929

Construction Commences on Power Station A

1944

Power Station B Becomes Operational

1975

Power Station A Closes

1980

Awarded Grade II Listed Status

1983

Power Station B Closes and First Competition for Reuse Proposal

2007	**2012**	**2013**	**2021**	**2022**
Awarded Grade II* Listed Status	Site Purchase by Malaysia Consortium	Restorative Work Begins on Site	1st Resident Moves in to the Power Station	Power Station Opens to Public

'Returning to the station, my first impressions were how magnificent it looks, particularly the chimneys, which really stand out now. It used to be called 'The Cathedral of Power' and it has retained that status.'

Jim Barnes, former Assistant Shift Charge Engineer
(1967 – 1969) at the Power Station

1935–1983
A Super Power Station for the Golden Age of Electricity

Constructed over two phases, the first completed in 1935 and the second in 1944, Battersea Power Station operated as a power station for just under 50 years before its closure in 1983. It would stand derelict for almost 40 years – a monument to London's industrial decline – before its transformation, renovation and reopening in October 2022.

One of the first 'Super Power Stations.' Battersea was built following a parliamentary recommendation in the mid 1920s for a publicly owned national electrical grid to serve the increasing use of electricity in Great Britain by both businesses and homes. To mollify genteel Chelsea and Pimlico residents across the river, who had voiced concerns around the construction of an imposing and polluting Power Station on their doorstep, the London Power Company commissioned architect and industrial designer, Sir Giles Gilbert Scott, famed for the red telephone box, as consulting architect for the exterior of this 'cathedral to electric power.'

Historic photo of engineers working on the turbines.
Image - Daily Herald Archive/Getty

1930s – The first stage of the Power Station, Battersea A, is completed. The top of the western pair of chimneys are 101m from the ground. The chimneys themselves are 50m each, while the wash towers they sit on are 51m. Image - Fox Photos/Getty

Built in 1935, the first phase of the building (Power Station A), including Turbine Hall A and Control Room A, reflects the golden era of electricity in which it was born and the calibre of the highly qualified technical staff who would walk its floors. Its lavish Art Deco interiors, designed by Halliday & Agate, include bespoke shapes and forms, along with expensive finishes including marble, teak parquet, bronze panels to entrance doors and gold painted window frames. The level of sophistication found in the detailing and materials is similar to that typically found in high-end hotels, residential properties or major corporate headquarter of the same period. At the cutting edge of technology at the time, anyone working in the electricity industry was well-respected and their working environment reflected this status.

above Historic photos of Control Room A.
Image - Fox Photos/Getty

1940s – The fourth chimney, and second stage of the Power Station is complete, with the Power Station at peak capacity. The space within the main Boiler House is so vast that it would be possible to fit St Paul's Cathedral within the space. Image - Fox Photos/Getty

left Power Station completed mid 50's.
Image - Monty Fresco/Getty

right Engineer at work in Turbine Hall B,
Battersea Power Station, Christmas Day, 1960
© Bridget Bishop / bridgetbishop.co.uk

Power Station B was completed during the Second World War becoming operational in 1944. While externally it mirrors the first phase - completing its famous four chimney form - the interior treatment stands in contrast to its glamorous predecessor. During this period, electric power stations had become part of everyday life and the designs for Turbine Hall B and Control Room B took on a more utilitarian form. Reflecting the modernist architecture of the 1950s, it incorporates big span structures and simple materials such as steel and concrete, with walls clad in standard, generously sized, faience tiles.

The pragmatism of this utilitarian architecture is particularly evident on the east elevation of Power Station B where, two thirds of the way down the elevation, there is a visible change of brick colour, marking the point in the build where they were forced to change supplier and simply accept the mismatch.

1983–2011
A Derelict Enigma

By the 1970s, technology had moved on significantly and, deemed too expensive and inefficient to run, Power Station A was decommissioned and ceased operation. In 1983, this was followed by the closure of Power Station B. And so began a 39 year hiatus during which time its future use was in constant question.

This vast facility, arguably the largest brick building in Europe (within a single envelope), posed a conundrum. Coupled with its scale, its interiors suffered from a total lack of natural light and poor transport links to the rest of London. These limiting factors to its redevelopment and renovation were further complicated when, in 1980, The Power Station was awarded with Grade II Listing (upgraded to Grade II* in 2007).

Over the twilight years of the 20th century, the building was purchased by and sold to numerous developers and celebrities, with almost every leading architect in London and beyond making proposals for its use; these ranged from wild and wonderful football stadia and theme parks to sensitive and civic parks and museums.

In the meantime, the building - which had always been extraordinary on the London skyline - took on iconic status. Part of London's recognisable cityscape, the Power Station could be viewed at a distance from the riverbank to the north, from Nine Elms Lane to the south or from the train tracks arriving into London from the south-west or (for a period of time) on the Eurostar as it arrived into Waterloo Station, acting as a beacon signifying one's arrival into the capital.

Set far back from the road and largely inaccessible by the public, this enigmatic cathedral was further entrenched in the Londoner's psyche by its constant reference in popular culture and advertising: for artists and marketeers alike, it offered a dynamic location to capture the imagination and, as such, was used as a location for a spectacular array of events, photoshoots, films and product launches.

The commercial opportunities the building offered to the advertising and events industry did not, however, translate into a commercially viable plan for the building's restoration, which had reached a critical stage. Already damaged by pollution of its own making, the building was further dilapidated in 1987, when most of the roof of the Boiler House's main volume was removed by its owners in preparation for its transformation to a theme park. When this development did not go ahead, the building was left derelict and open to the elements. Before long it was in ruin and the potential costs for its restoration astronomical.

left Prime Minister Margaret Thatcher visits a derelict Battersea Power Station in 1988 Image - PA Images/Alamy

right Poster from Battersea Power Station Community Group, critical of a proposed theme park scheme Image - BrianBarnes/BPSCG

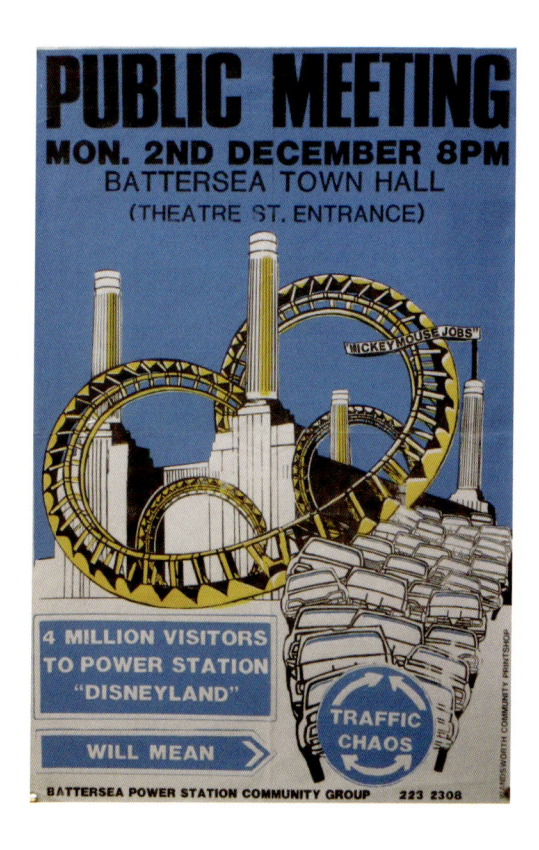

In October 2013, the Power Station was opened up for the weekend as part of the Open House Festival, offering the public one last chance to visit before works commenced

Battersea Power Station is industry made civic. It's a carbon-belching brute turned national monument that once burned 240 tons of coal per hour and electrified 20 percent of London, before entering a long retirement as the backdrop of album covers, films, fashion shoots and the everyday life of the capital. Also as the country's biggest heritage problem, passing through British, Chinese, Irish and Malaysian owners, and numerous proposals by leading architects and consultancy teams, each trying to work out how to make a commercial proposition out of the expensive-to-fix hulk, which nonetheless was listed Grade II*.

Battersea Power Station: a giant that needs no grand gestures,
Rowan Moore, *The Observer*, Sun 9 Oct 2022

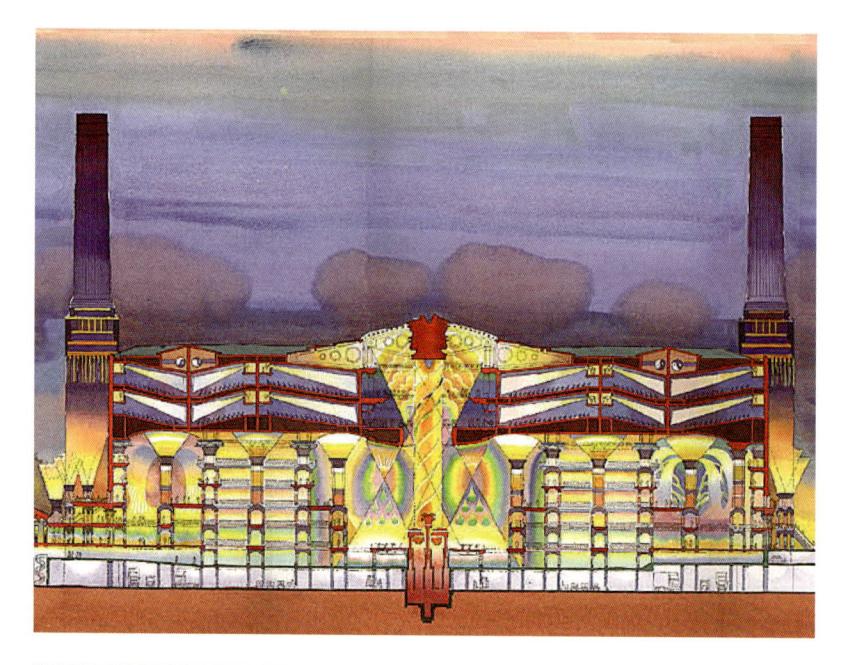

Unrealised Designs

From a giant roller coaster around a museum of architecture to the new home for Chelsea Football Club; a museum of industry to a theme park; a luxury hotel to a simple park in the middle of the building left in ruin; proposals for the Power Station have never failed to fuel the collective imagination, each one raising expectations from year to year of what the final redevelopment might be.

top John Outram Associates scheme full of ambition and psychedelic colour

bottom A park within a building proposal by Terry Farrell. Image - Farrells

In Popular Culture

During its almost 40-year closure, the Power Station formed the backdrop to many movies including classics such as *The Dark Knight*, *Superman*, *The King's Speech* and *RocknRolla*. It also served as a fantastic venue for concerts, motorbike races, open air light displays, catwalk shows and product launches. Most famously, perhaps, it appears on the cover of Pink Floyd's 'Animals' album.

top Pink Floyd's infamous 'Animals' album artwork recreated 35 years later. Image - Joseph Toth/Alamy

bottom Red Bull X-Fighters event in the grounds of the Power Station. Image - European Sports Photo Agency/Alamy

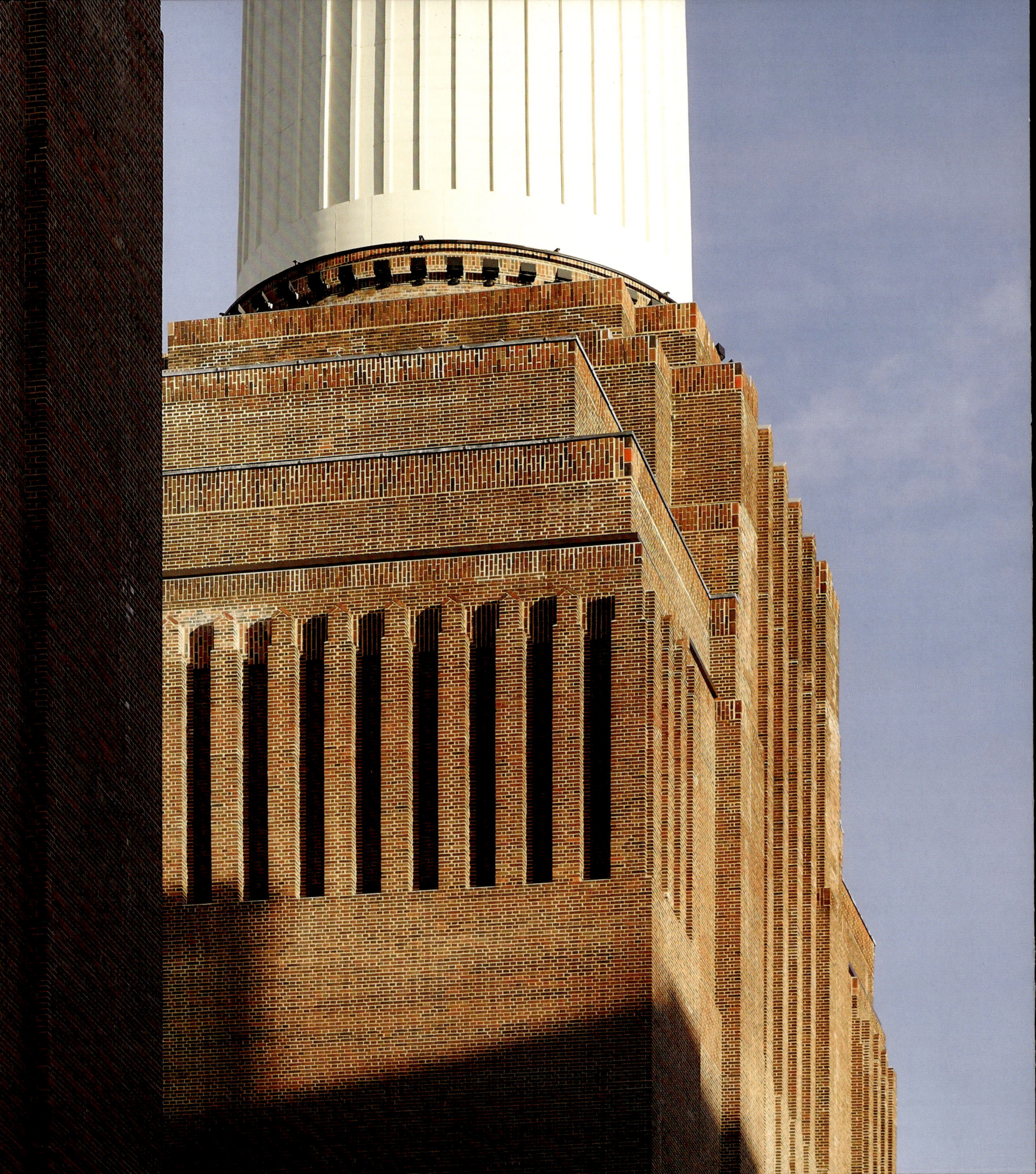

How do you solve a problem like Battersea Power Station?

2

A Modern Ruin

Despite its relative youth in heritage terms, The Power Station's 30-year neglect had created a modern ruin which posed a considerably more difficult redevelopment challenge than any medieval castle or Victorian family seat. By 2012, the Power Station was in a critical state of disrepair and had been on the Heritage at Risk Register since 1995: the main roof was missing, some of the key walls had collapsed and the site was contaminated with asbestos, hydrocarbons and lead paint. The existing structure was not fire rated and there was very little remaining within the 50m height main volume.

The Power Station's 'national treasure' status, coupled with its Grade II* Listing, spawned a romantic desire among many to see it reimagined as a cultural building or for social housing: noble ideas which, unfortunately, did not stack up. London already had a Power Station which had been converted to a cultural centre in the form of the Tate Modern, completed in 2000. At an enormous three times the size of the Bankside Power Station which had given the Tate it's home, another solution needed to be found for Battersea.

Under Irish group REO, Rafael Viñoly was commisioned to develop a viable masterplan which reframed the Power Station as part of a wider neighbourhood. The plan included improved infrastructure via an extension to the underground's Northern Line and connections with nearby developments at Nine Elms, including the US Embassy and New Covent Garden Market. After the masterplan gained outline planning consent in 2010/11, the site was purchased by a consortium of Malaysian investors in 2012, who established Battersea Power Station Development Company to manage the development.

Following a design competition, WilkinsonEyre Architects were appointed in 2013 with the remit to deliver an exemplary restoration of the building's heritage features complemented by high quality new architecture within Viñoly's masterplan context.

Early watercolour sketch by
Chris Wilkinson

above South elevation in 2013

opposite Detail of main elevation between the washtowers in 2013

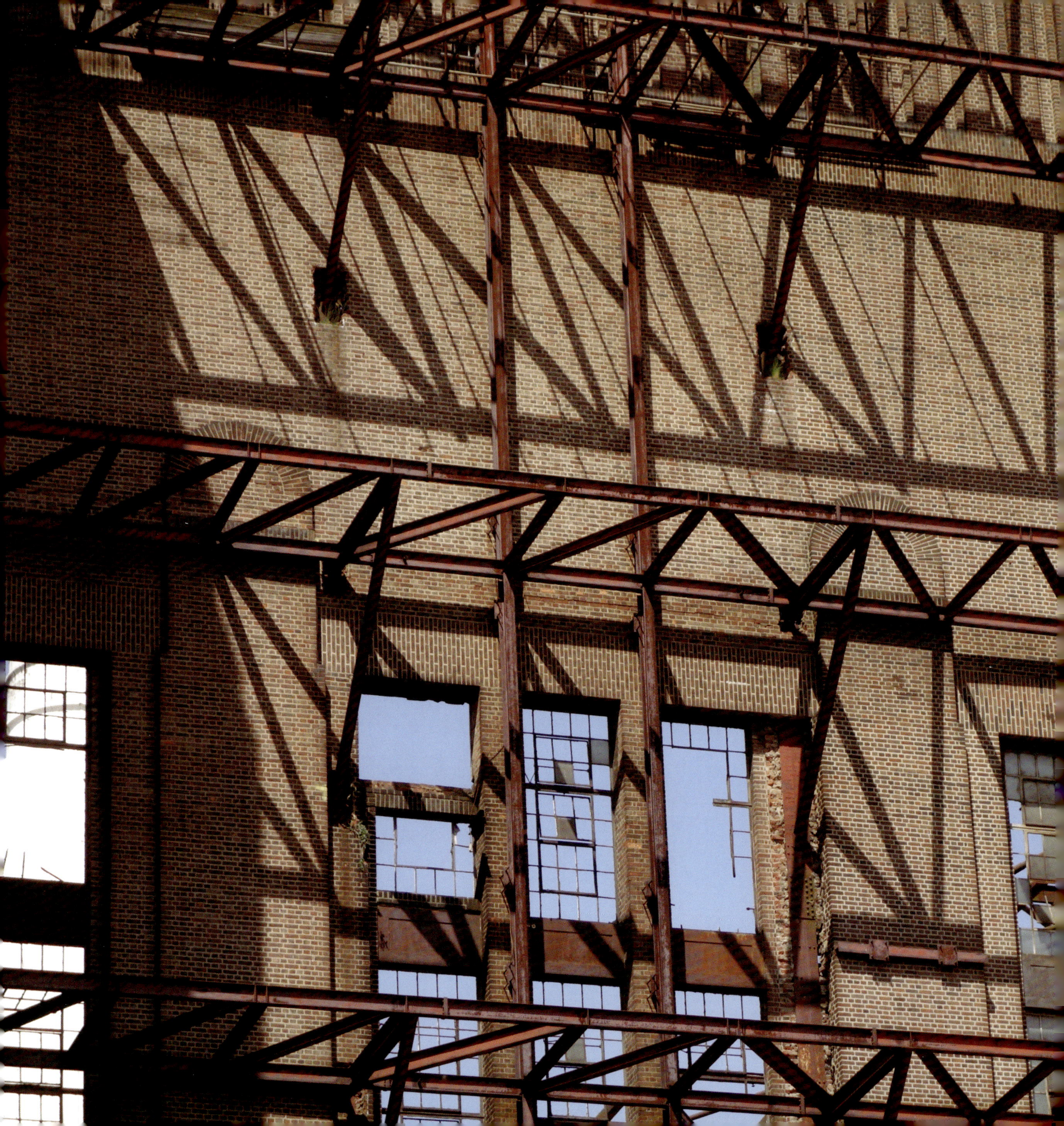

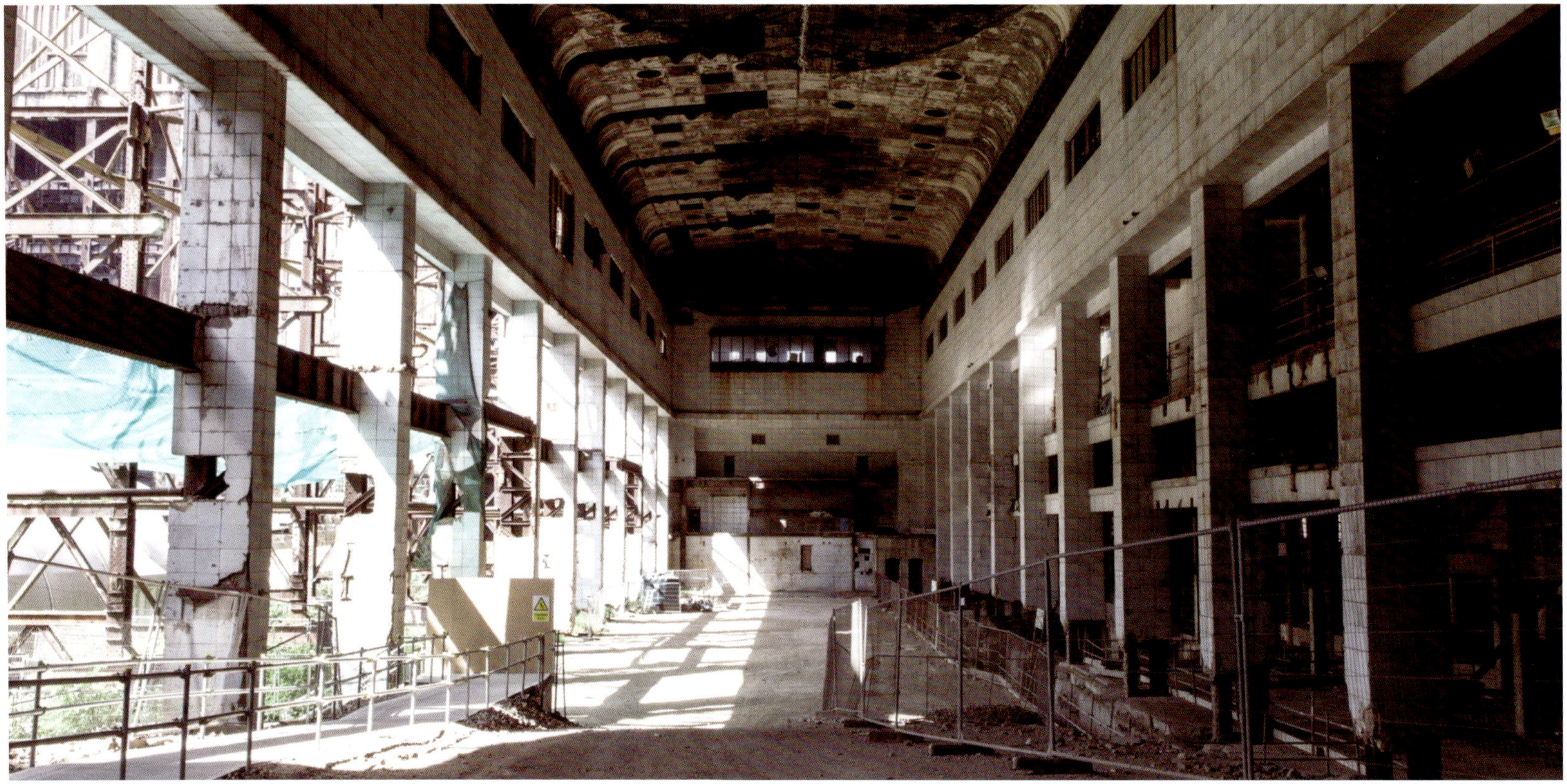

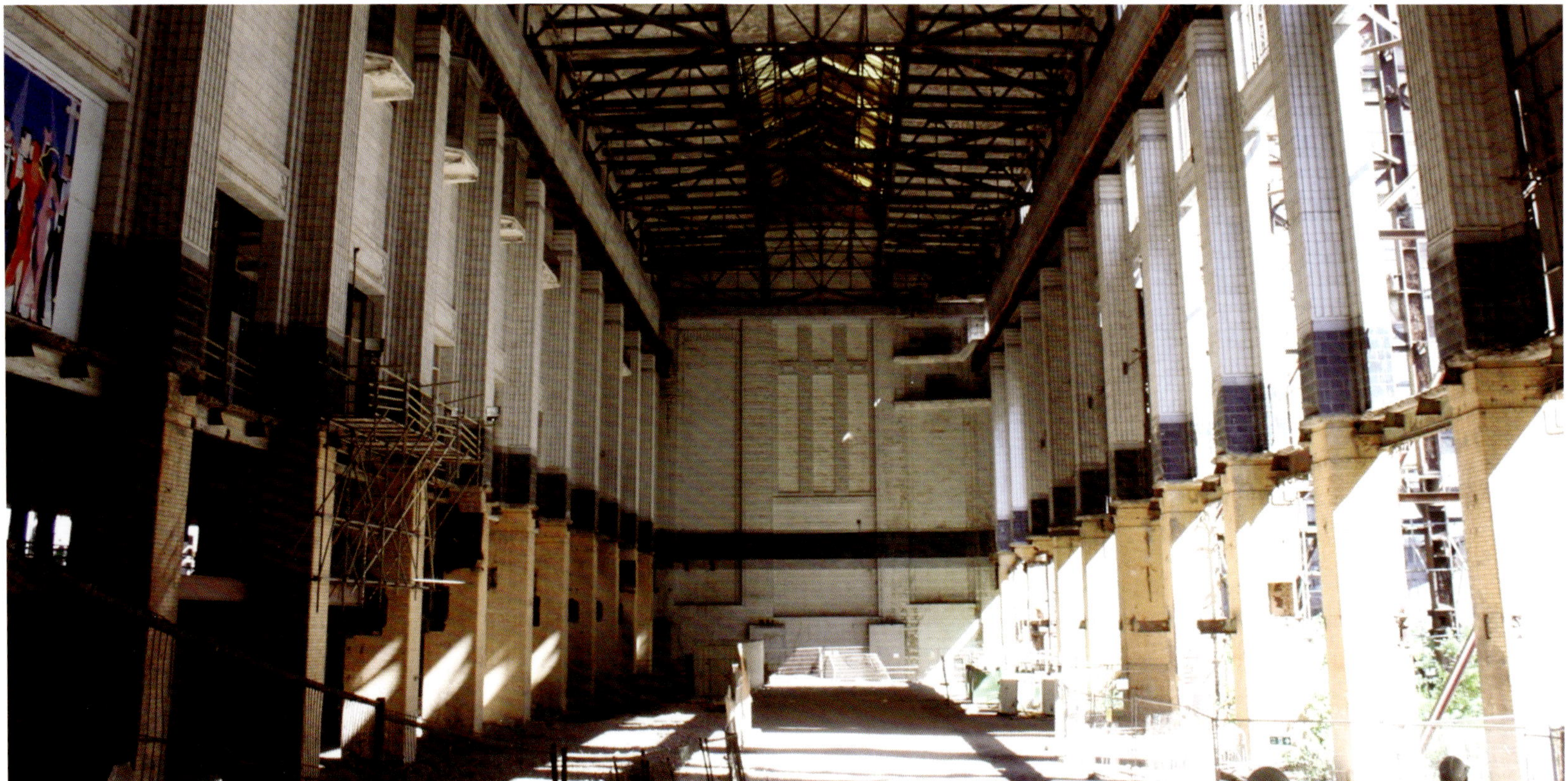

opposite Turbine Hall B and Turbine Hall A in 2013

above Control Room A and the control panels in Control Room B

'Whilst mammoth in scale, The Power Station typifies the problems shared by most modern industrial Listed Buildings in the UK: heavily contaminated and poorly maintained, it was designed for a process, not for human beings. To assure a sustainable and commercially viable future for the building, therefore, our approach to the historic fabric had to be one of sensitive transformation rather than faithful renovation.'

Sebastien Ricard,
WilkinsonEyre

Retaining the Magic

WilkinsonEyre's brief was very clear from the outset: to do justice to the Power Station's historic architecture and retain its magic, whilst making it a sustainable and accessible new district for Londoners. The practice's early concept sketches highlight its fundamental approach to achieving this: one which retains the Power Station's sense of scale and visual drama by revealing the building's full height elevation and chimney, and one that does not 'over-restore' and ensures any interventions are stepped away from the existing fabric.

It was important to both the Architects and BPSDC that future occupiers and visitors would be able to read and recognise the history of the building as a Power Station. As such, new interventions are lightweight in form to avoid breaking the building's scale and visual links to the chimneys and the existing fabric are prioritised throughout. Coupled with these macro moves, the practice was to take a detail-oriented and celebratory approach to the restoration. In places, existing equipment has been reinstated, used as urban sculpture within the building or in its surrounding public realm.

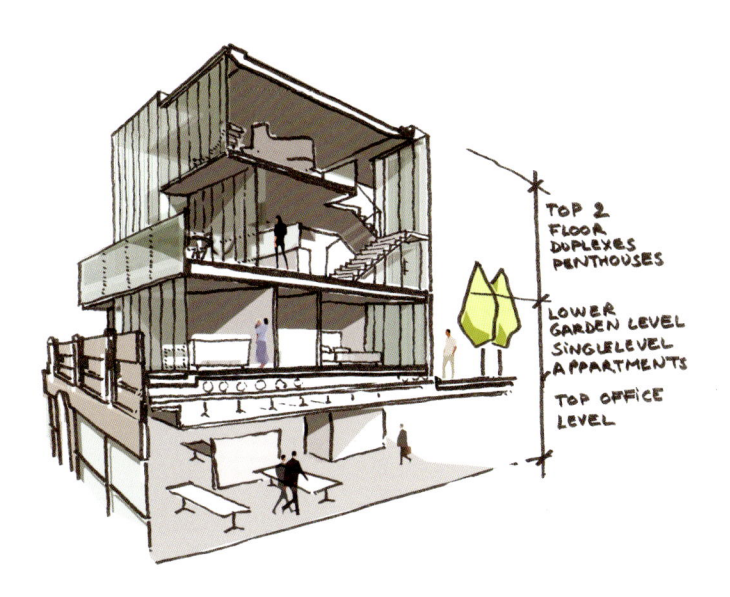

left Generous green space on the roof and 'Villas in the Sky' formed part of the early design concept

above Early concept sketch of South Entrance, showing full height atrium with exposed historic fabric and view to the chimney

The Masterplan

Battersea Power Station Development Company's (BPSDC) masterplan for the site has developed from the 2010 scheme by Rafael Viñoly. It transforms a vast industrial brownfield site to a new community of homes, shops, bars, restaurants, cafes and offices, with almost half of its 42 acres given over to public space.

The key diagram sets out a series of radial developments around the Power Station, set away from the historic building by a well-defined circular road - nicknamed 'Halo Road'- which guarantees a minimum distance between the Listed fabric and new buildings. The masterplan's other key principle was to retain open space between the Power Station and the river, maintaining important perspectives and uninterrupted views to the north elevation of the building. Other key aspects of the masterplan include a height restriction to all surrounding buildings, keeping them below the height of the base of the Power Station's chimneys.

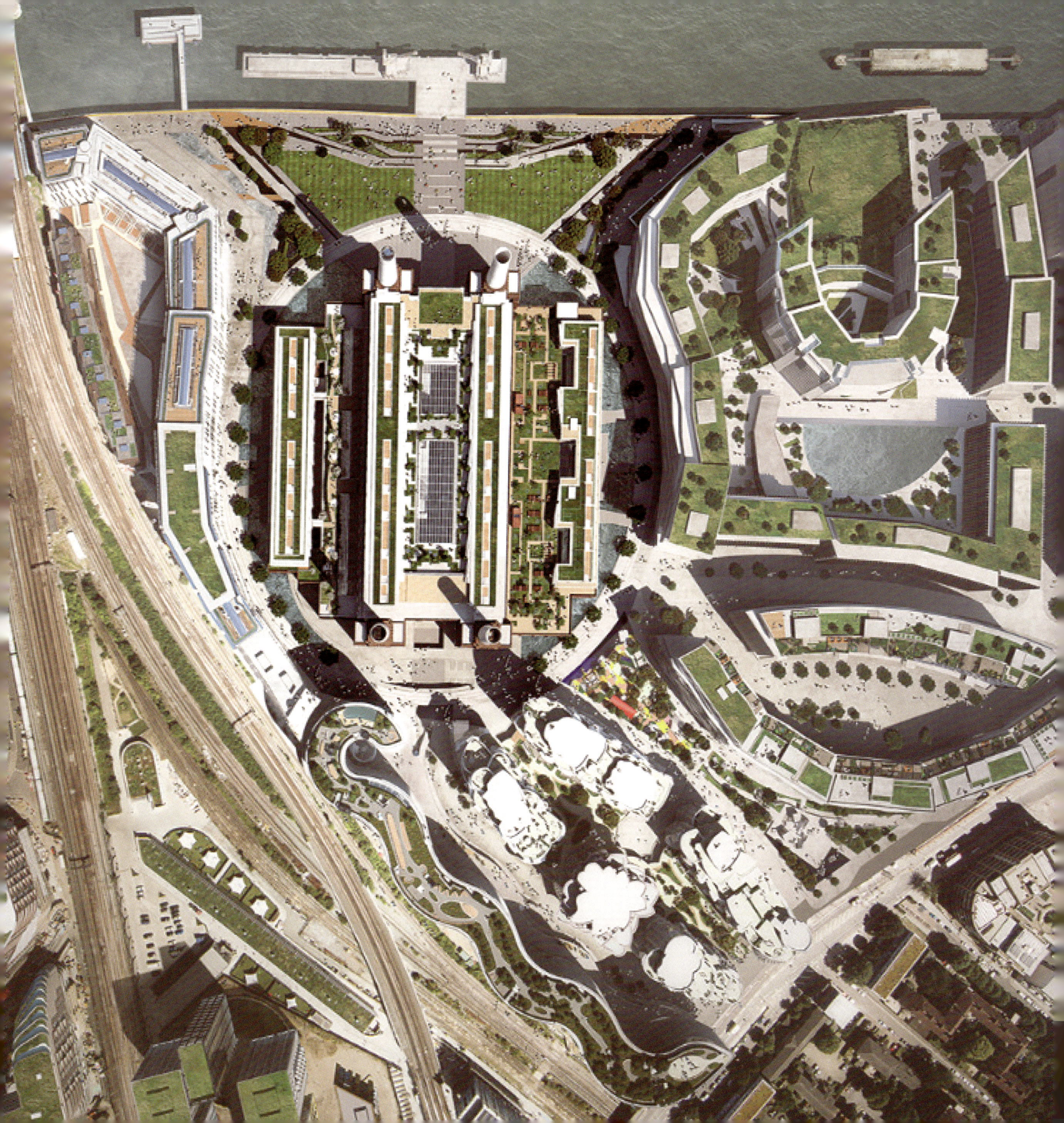

'It's a listed building. There are lots of unknowns - technical and other challenges that you find out as it progresses. The integration of all the different uses (residential, retail, leisure, office) in one building is unusual in this country.'

Jim Eyre,
Director, WilkinsonEyre

A Town within a Building

WilkinsonEyre were commissioned to design Phase Two of eight phases in the wider development, with a scope including the Grade II* Listed building in its entirety, with a curtilage that extended to the circular 'Halo Road' around the heritage asset, and the new park between the building and the river. The practice's design creates a truly mixed-use building incorporating approximately 35,000 m2 of retail (around 120 shops), approximately 45,000 m2 of office over six storeys (equivalent to 'The Gherkin'), 254 homes, an event space for 1500 people, and a multiplex cinema.

In addition to the Power Station itself, the practice was charged with the design of the below grade infrastructure for the overall masterplan which was contained within a three-storey basement under North Park and in between the building and the 'Halo Road'. These spaces include car parking, service loading bays, a servicing road and a 6,000 sqm energy centre serving all phases of the new development.

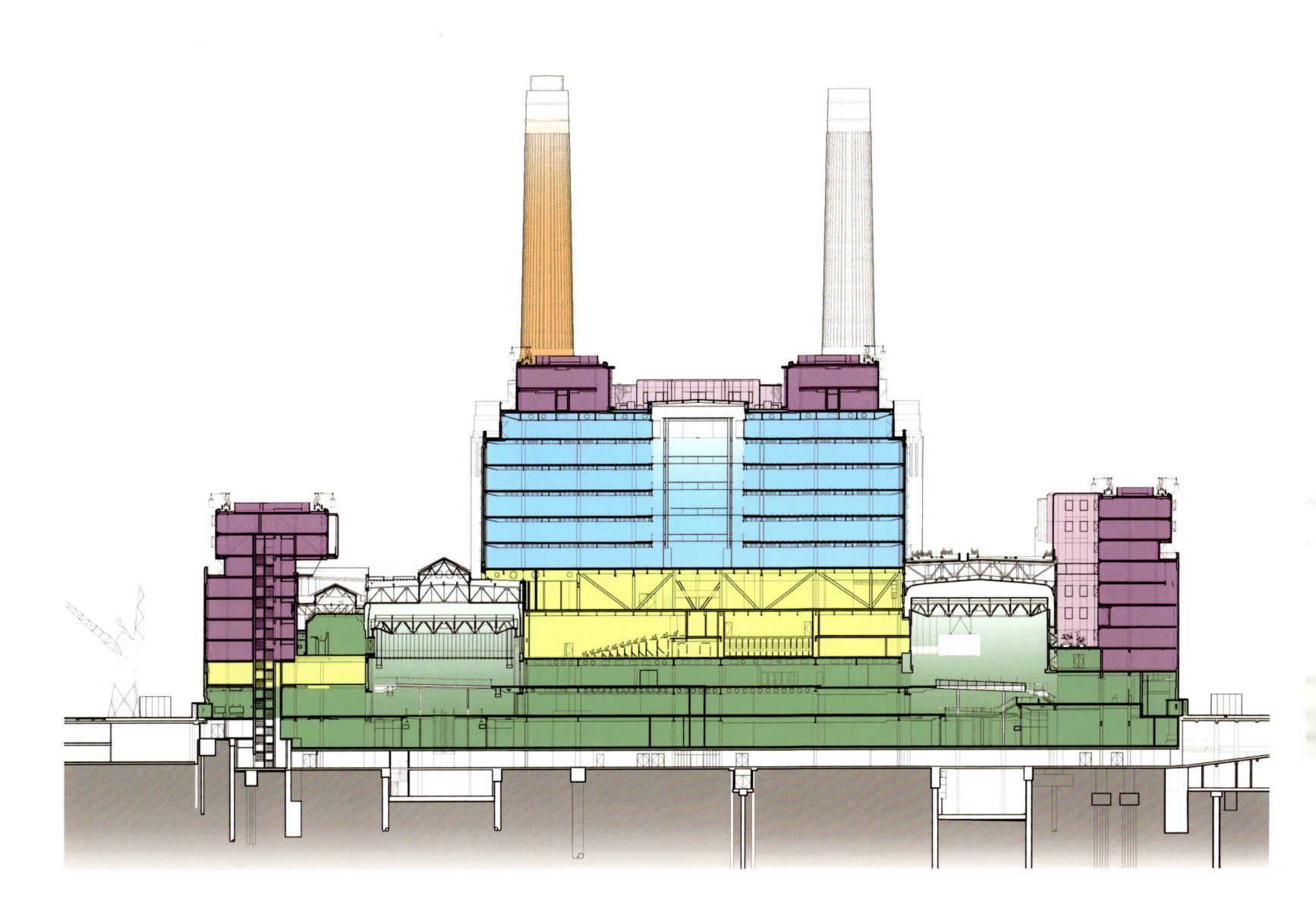

Cross section indicating the mix of activities inside the building

- Chimney Lift
- Residential Access
- Office Access
- Retail Access
- Leisure Access

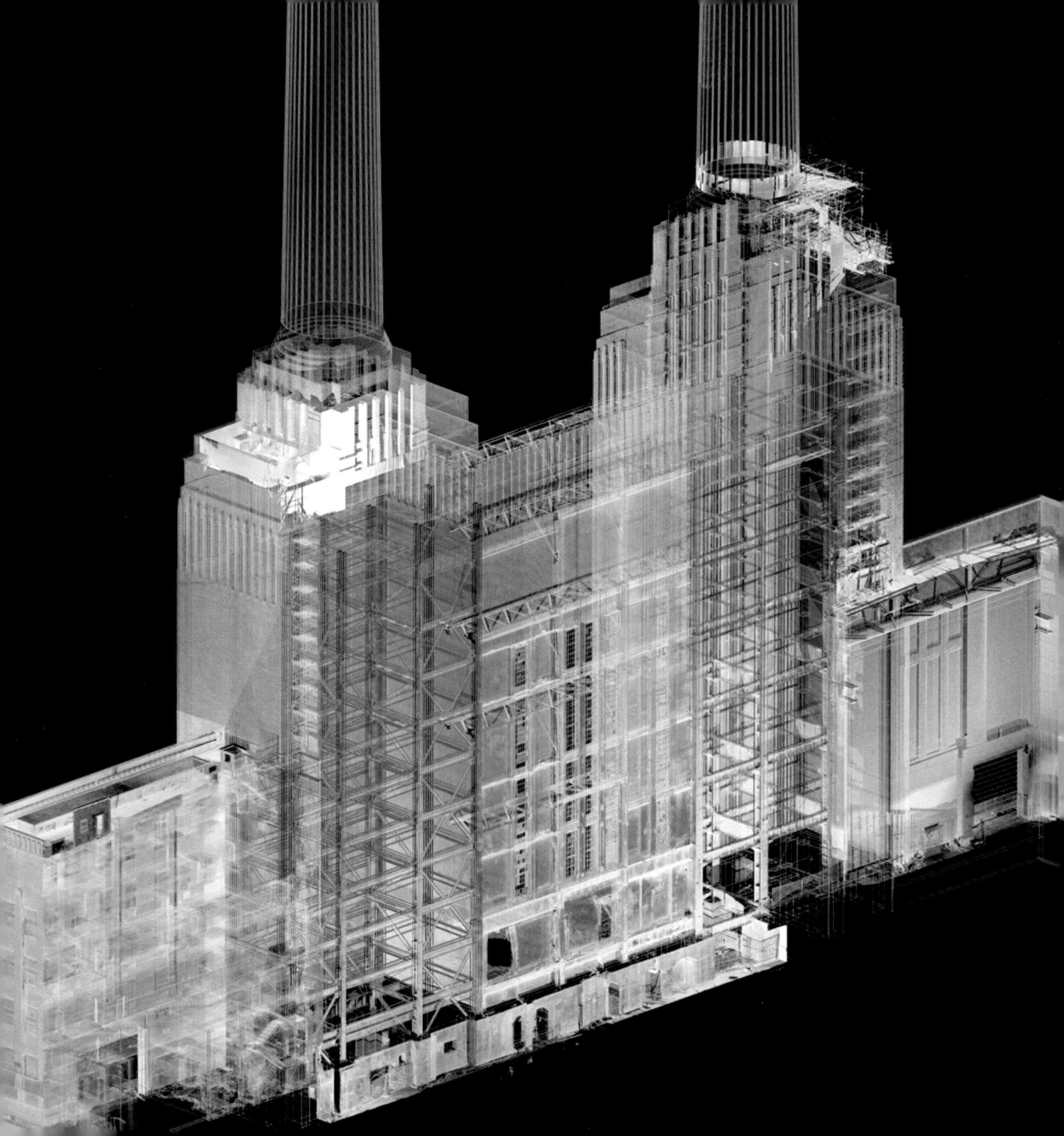

Learning the Building
Cataloguing the Existing

3

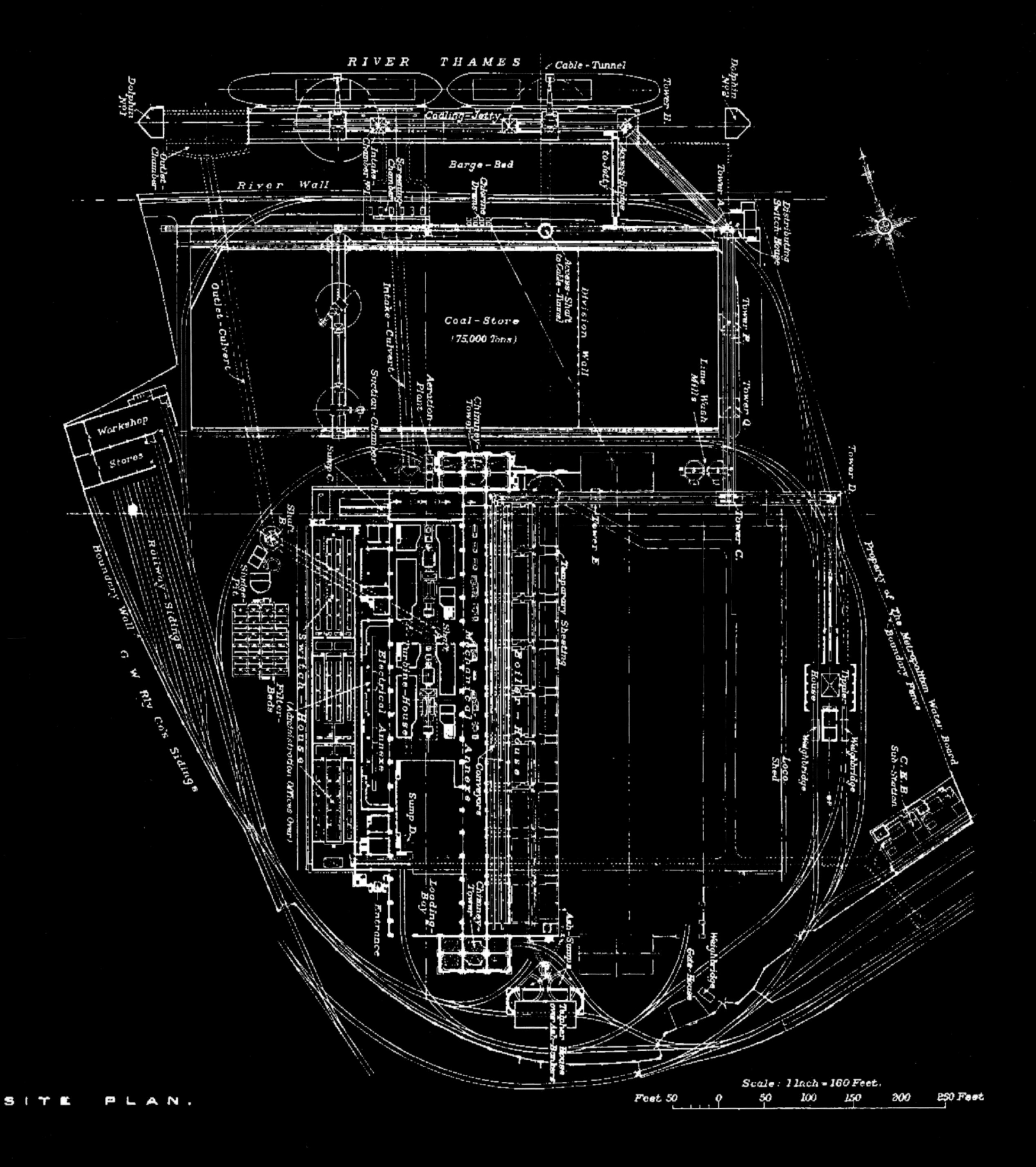

SITE PLAN.

Scale: 1 Inch = 160 Feet.

PLAN AT GROUND-LEVEL.

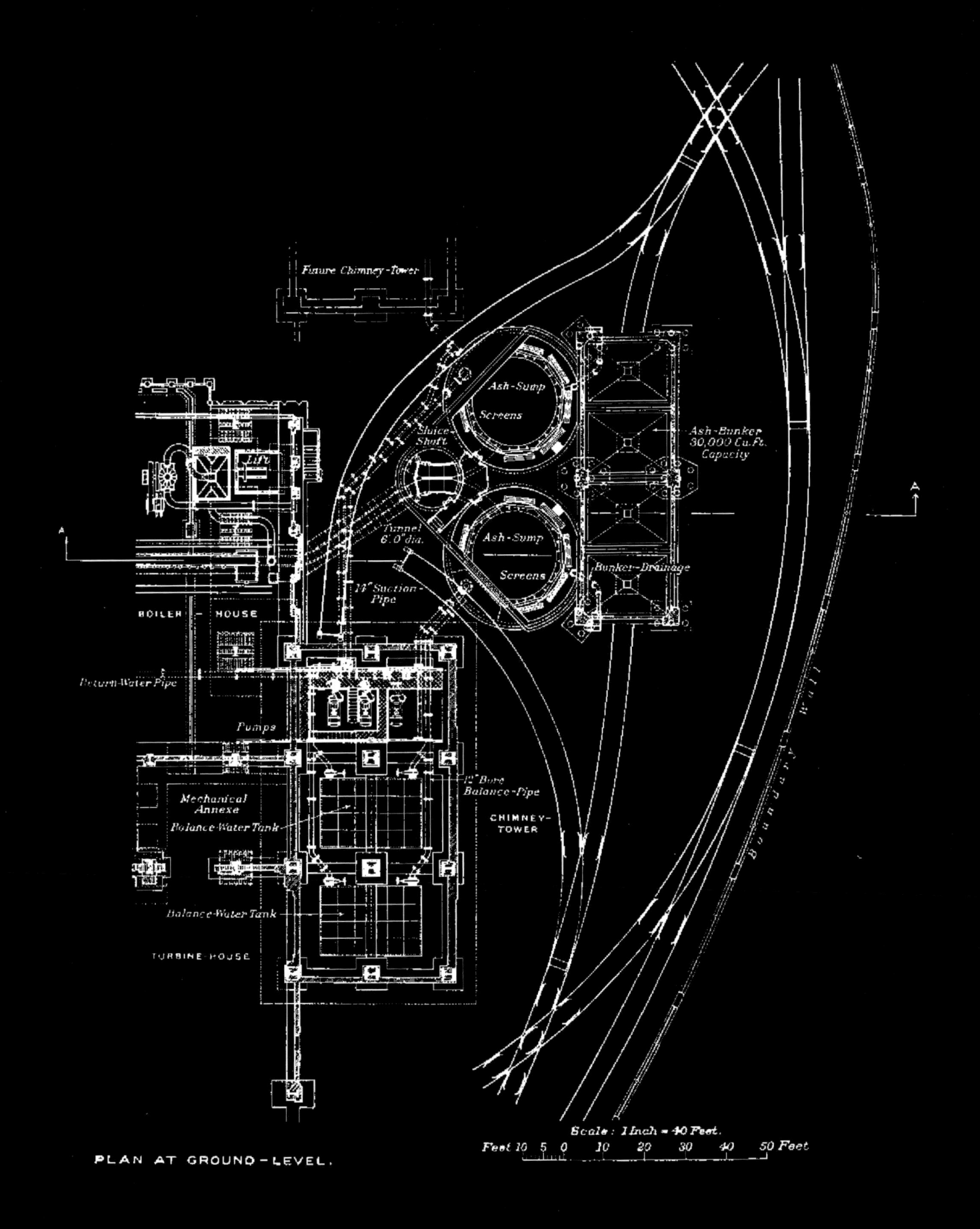

Scale: 1 Inch = 40 Feet.

Coal-Transporte

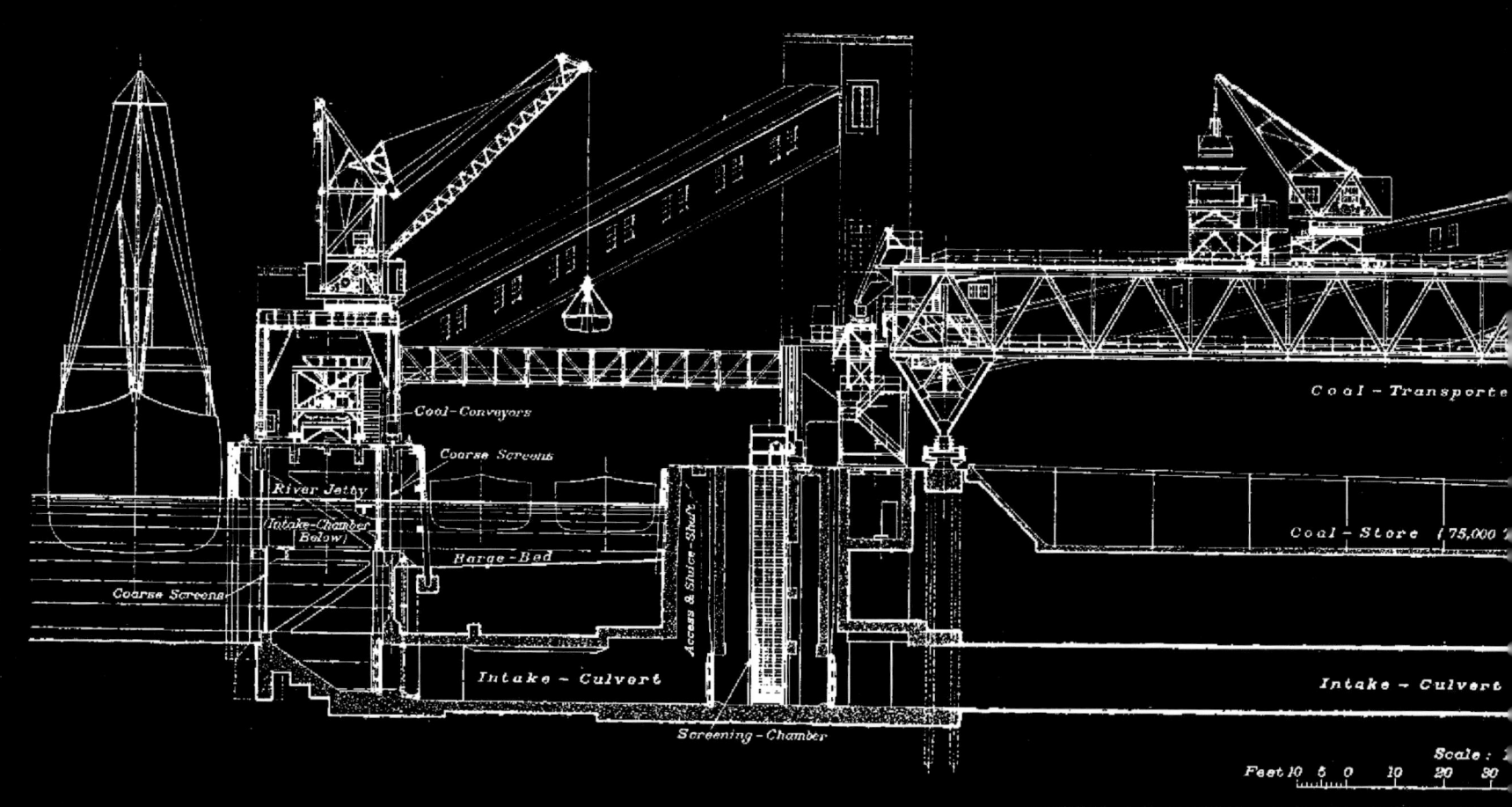

Coal-Conveyors

Coarse Screens

River Jetty

Intake-Chamber
(Below)

Barge-Bed

Coal - Store (75,000 T

Coarse Screens

Access & Sluice-Shaft

Intake - Culvert

Intake - Culvert

Screening-Chamber

Scale:
Feet 10 5 0 10 20 30

GENERAL LONGITUDINAL SECTION ALONG LINE O

E-CULVERT AND TURBINE-HOUSE (NORTH END)

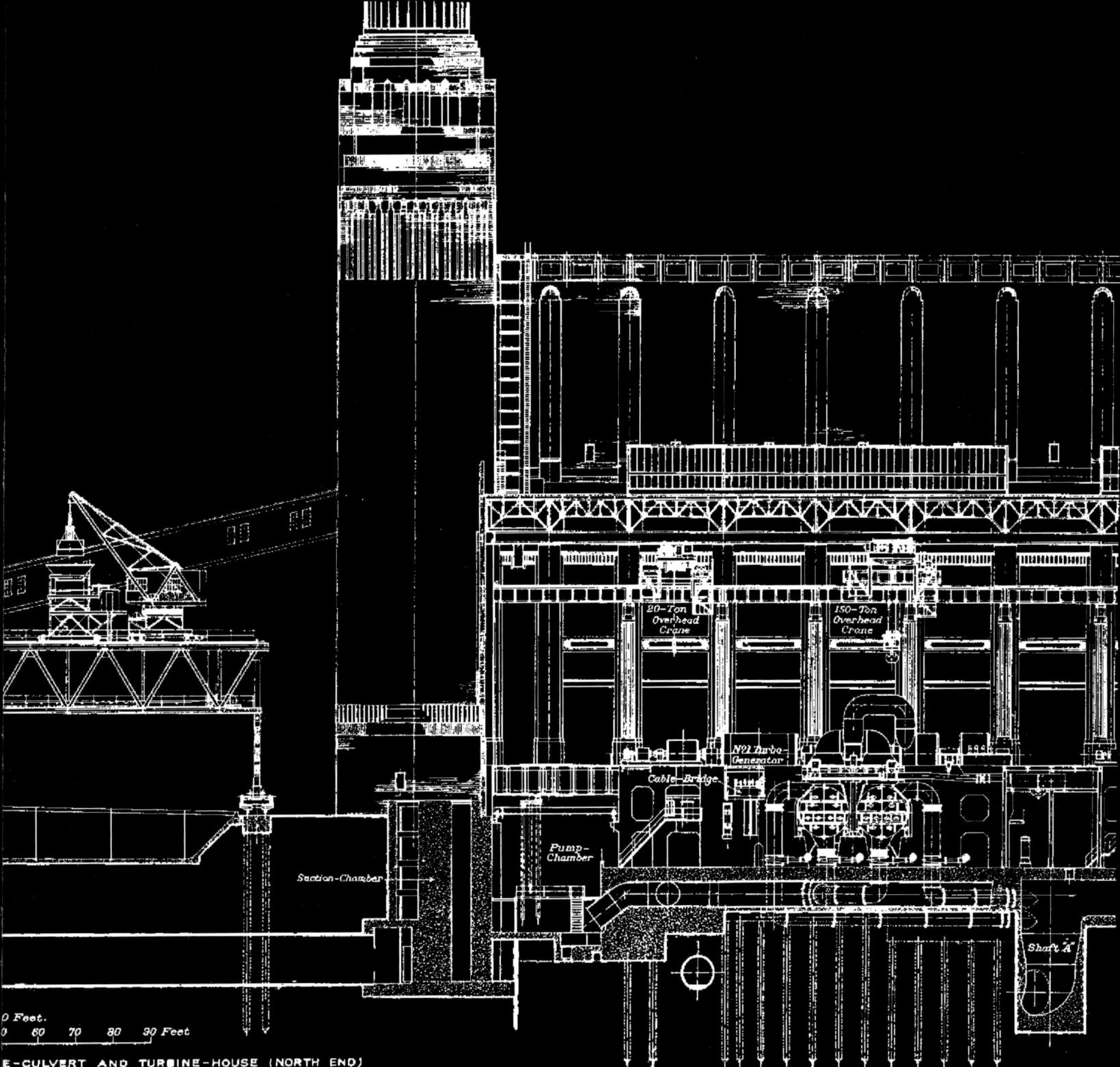

20-Ton Overhead Crane
150-Ton Overhead Crane
No.1 Turbo-Generator
Cable-Bridge
Pump-Chamber
Suction-Chamber
Shaft "A"

opposite Photos of the existing fabric

Cataloguing the Existing

WilkinsonEyre began the renovation of the Power Station by undertaking a thorough analysis of the existing site and structure. Whilst this type of research forms the first stage of any ordinary project, like so many elements of this monumental development, the scale and depth of the analysis of the Power Station was unprecedented on any scheme designed by the practice.

One of the first steps undertaken was to commission a 3D cloud survey of the building. Using specialist imaging software, a three-dimensional photographic report of the building fabric was produced recording the existing state of the Power Station.

This report formed the basis for a journalistic catalogue of restoration work, classifying the strategy, materials and technology required for the restoration of each existing component.

43

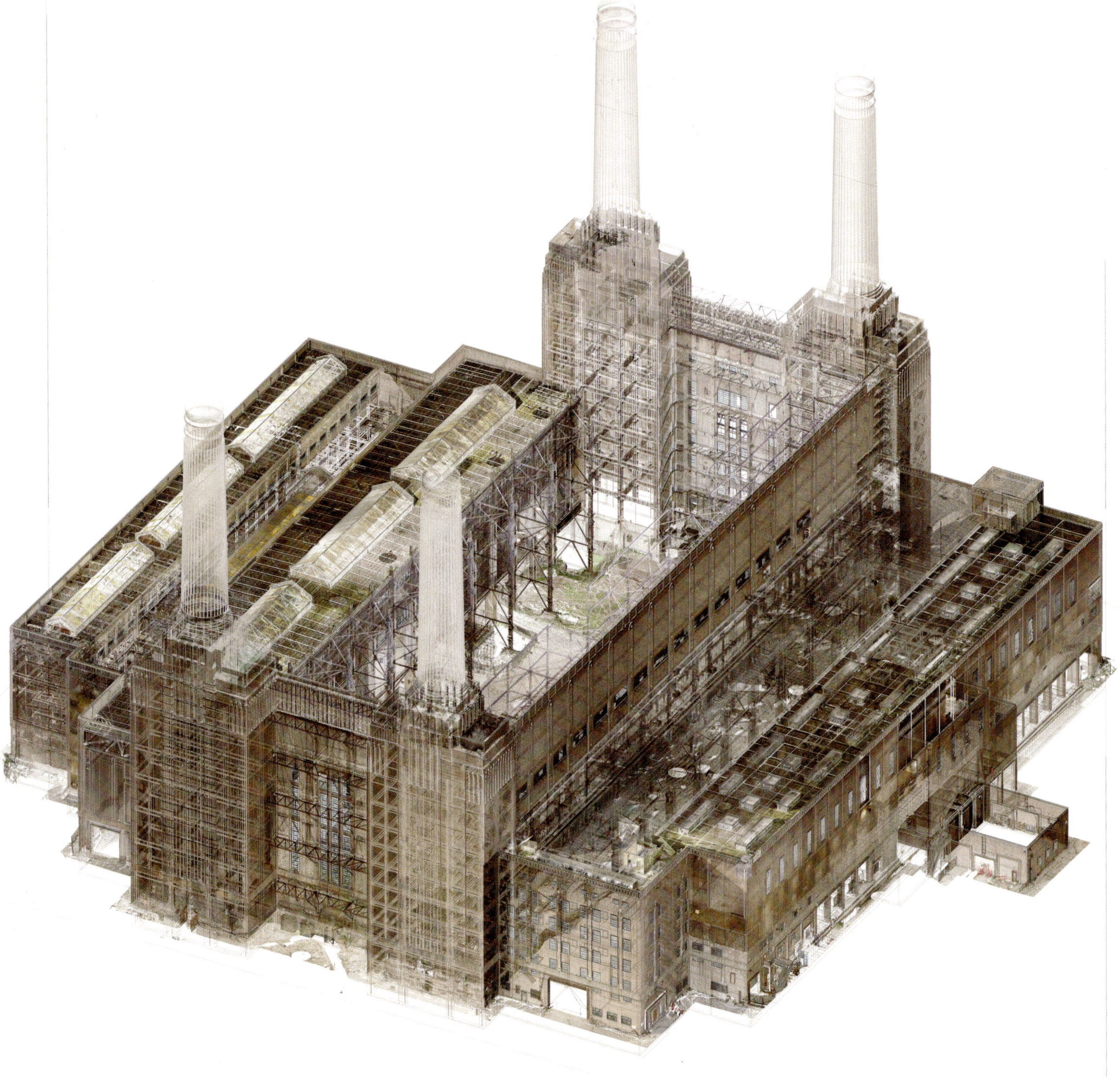

opposite Screenshot of the commissioned 3D cloud survey

above Extract from the 3D cloud survey of the staircase and adjacent rooms

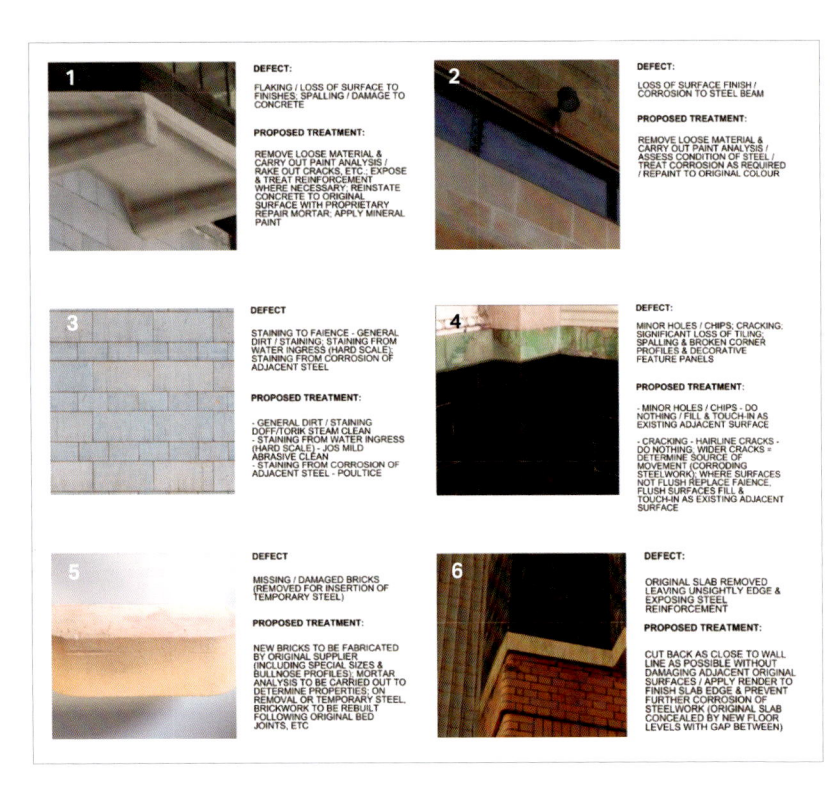

Restoration Strategy

The Power Station is comprised of a variety of structures of varying quality and special interest, built over 30 years so the restoration strategy considers the specific stories that could be told for each of these elements. The industrial scars of the utilitarian Boiler House are retained and exposed but then the severely damaged faience of Turbine Hall A has been repaired and reinstated to present the original Art Deco design. The Control Rooms and Director's Entrance with their fine finishes and intricate panels have required a painstakingly detailed assessment of condition with specialist conservation and repair to present them in their original glory.

The restoration followed common principles of conservation and repair but what made the challenge so extraordinary was the scale. Internal condition surveys of 35m high elevations had to be carried our by abseilers and across the internal walls, there are more than 15000 individually identified defects for which appropriate repairs were specified. Some of this could only be carried out as the new structural frame rose inside the building to provide access, so this was an even evolving process through construction.

The Turbine Hall A illustation shows how the overall repair strategy translates into the individual repairs to be carried out by specialist contractors.

The Turbine Hall B column example shows the poor condition and how defects had to be individually assessed to make sure that the repairs were appropriately specified for the trade contractors to achieve the overall vision.

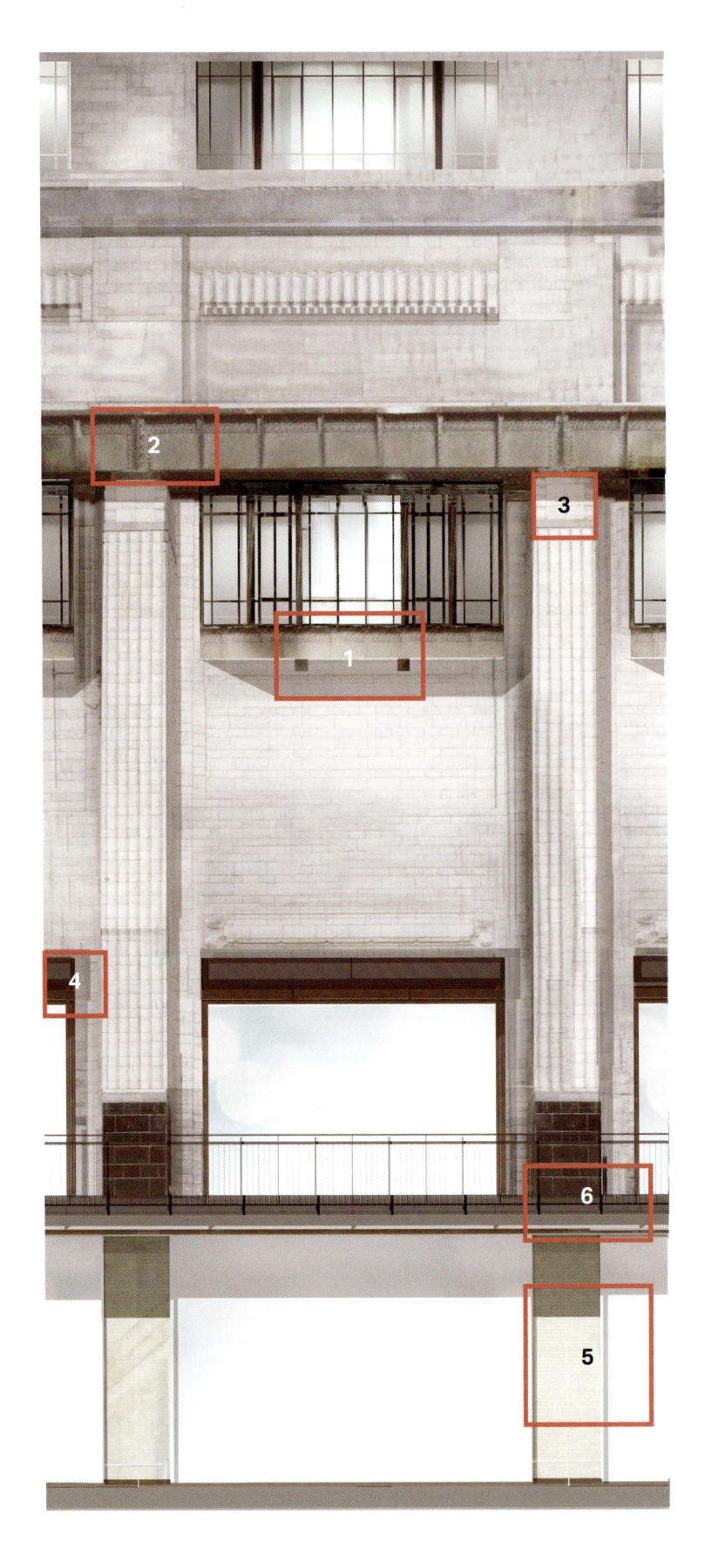

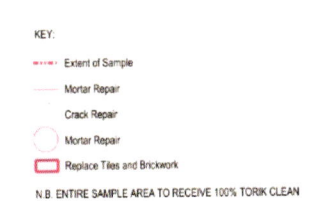

KEY:
- - - - Extent of Sample
——— Mortar Repair
——— Crack Repair
○ Mortar Repair
☐ Replace Tiles and Brickwork

N.B. ENTIRE SAMPLE AREA TO RECEIVE 100% TORIK CLEAN

RST1
Steel to be cut back and ground to project from faience no more than 10mm. Remaining exposed steel to receive intumescent paint finish. Surrounding faience to receive mortar repair

RT1A/RT7A
Resin based filler repair

RT1B
Tinted render repair

RT2A RT1C
Faience repairs: Remove all loose material back to sound substrate. Obtain replacement tile to match adjacent original tiles in dimensions, colour, pattern, density and profile fix using suitable proprietary adhesive and secure whilst setting. Repoint to match adjacent originals

RB4-RB5
Cut loose or damaged bricks to nearest complete unit with great caution to prevent damage to surrounding sound bricks. By using a fine, sharp chisel surrounding joints can be cut out and raked back before removing the failed brick, insert brick of type to match existing adjacent fully bedded in mortar to the approved mix/ specification into the wall.

RT1A
Mortar repair to crack

RA3A RT1A
Remove fixings
Mortar repair to make good

RT2A
Faience repairs: Remove all loose material back to sound substrate. Obtain replacement tile to match adjacent original tiles in dimensions, colour, pattern, density and profile fix using suitable proprietary adhesive and secure whilst setting. Repoint to match adjacent originals

RB4-RB5
Cut loose or damaged bricks to nearest complete unit with great caution to prevent damage to surrounding sound bricks. By using a fine, sharp chisel surrounding joints can be cut out and raked back before removing the failed brick, insert brick of type to match existing adjacent fully bedded in mortar to the approved mix/ specification into the wall.

opposite Turbine Hall A typical bay elevation

above Extract from WilkinsonEyre condition survey - record photos

47

A Huge Challenge: Navigating Scale

Once the initial analysis of the historic fabric was complete WilkinsonEyre could begin to consider the introduction of new interventions. Designed to house industrial-sized machinery, the Turbine Halls were each approximately 25m in width, 120m long and around 25m in height. The approach, therefore, to creating new elements within them brought multiple challenges of scale.

Without compromising the cathedral-like qualities which defined the existing building, the design needed to create spaces which were comfortable for humans to inhabit and enjoy. As such, the practice developed a 'box-in-a-box' approach, stepping back any interventions from the existing fabric and inserting independent structures to temper the vast volumes.

The mammoth scale of the development also posed practical and financial challenges in terms of delivery: coupled with the risk of tasking one contractor with any package of work for the entire project, very few contractors were even able to deliver a building as large and complex as a town on their own. As such, every element of the project was broken down into smaller and more manageable packages. The new cladding components, for example, were split between five contractors: Seele, Focchi, Thorp, Lesterose and OAG, where existing wall repairs were split between Paye/Szerelmey and Pyramid.

opposite Turbine Hall A in 2013. Window filled in and rooflights painted

49

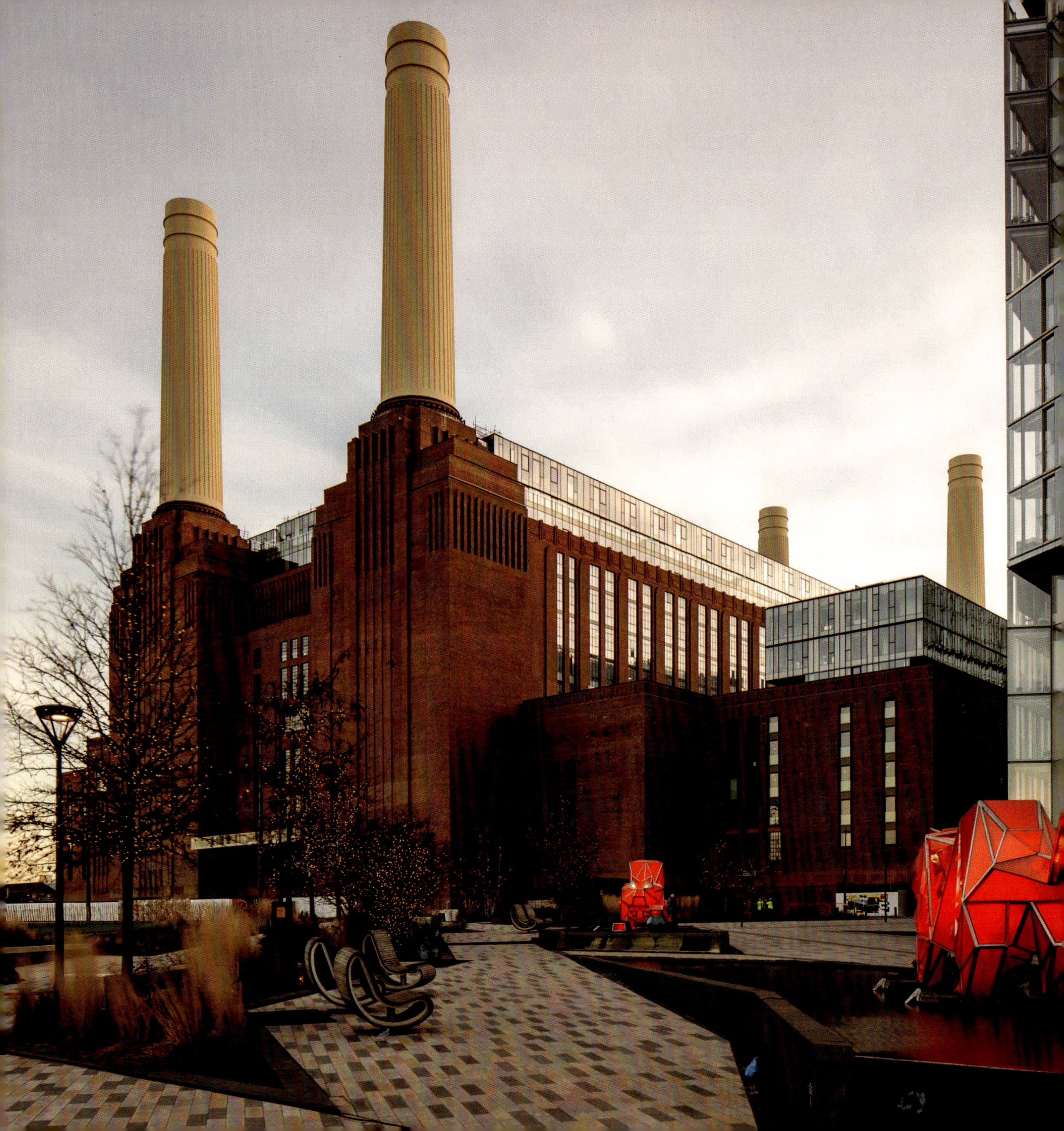

A Town in a Building
The Key Components

4

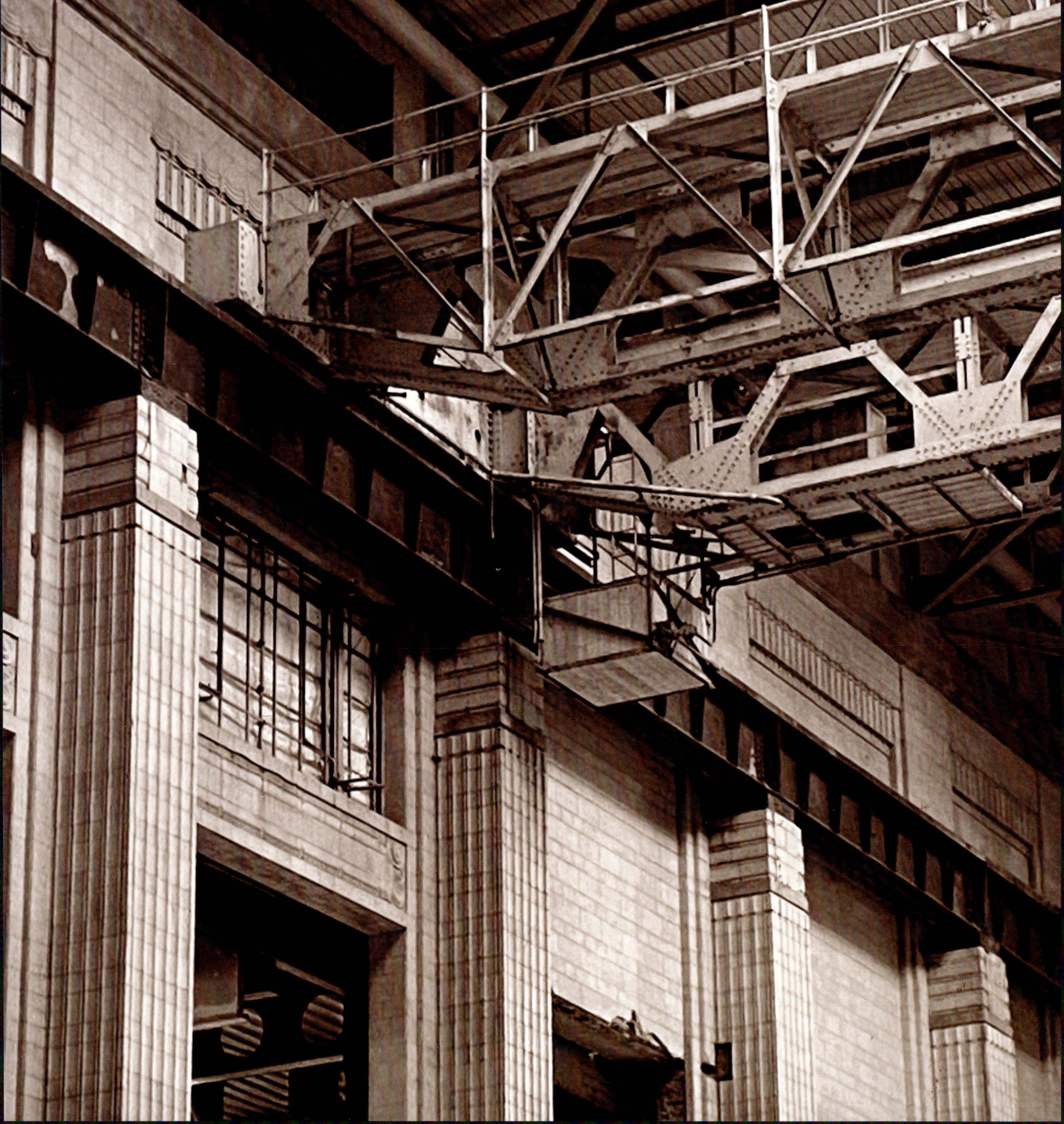

Retail

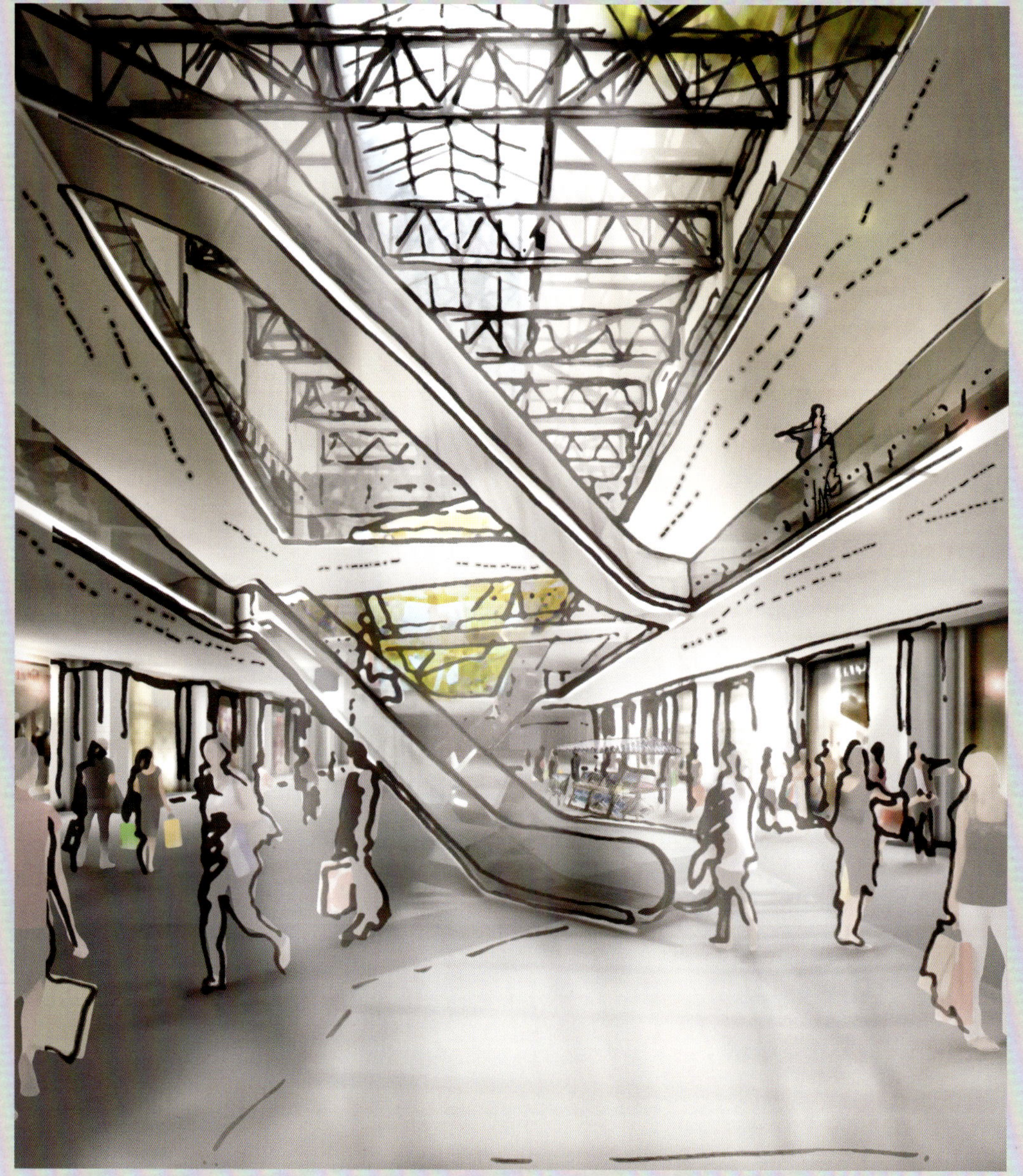

Retail access diagram

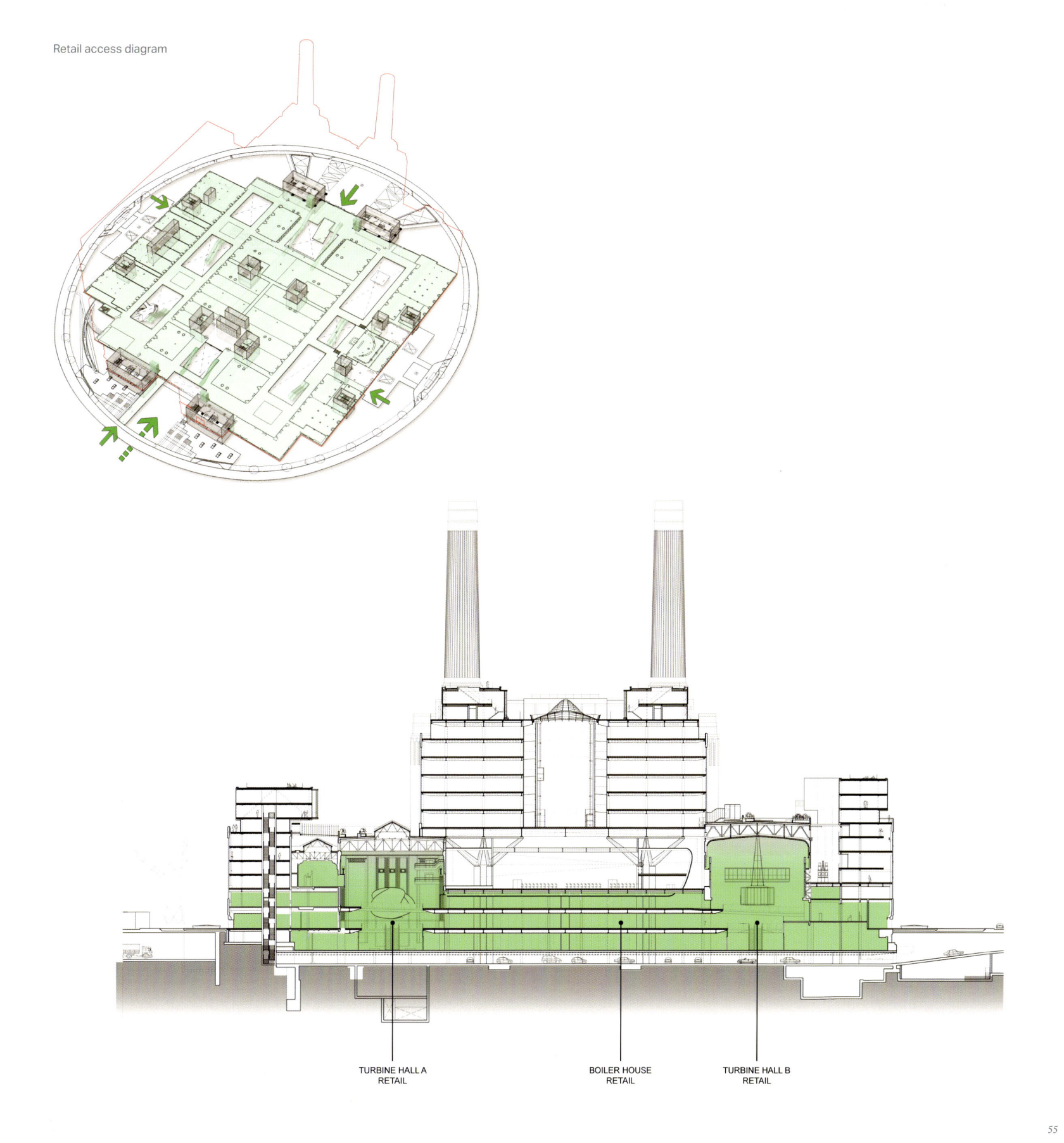

TURBINE HALL A RETAIL

BOILER HOUSE RETAIL

TURBINE HALL B RETAIL

55

Comprising some 350,000 sqft, including 120 shops, the retail component of the Power Station is equivalent in scale to some of London's largest shopping malls. As with so much of the project, the key challenges in designing the retail were to deliver human scale in a vast space and to be commercially successful whilst retaining the magic and history which make Battersea so unique. It was crucial that shoppers recognise they were in an old Power Station rather than a generic shopping precinct.

To temper the scale of the heroic turbine halls, vertical circulation and a series of lightweight walkways and bridges have been introduced, cutting across the space to create three storeys within each volume and maximising efficiency. These walkways have also enabled the provision of well-proportioned back-of-house services. To protect the Grade II* Listed building, none of these new components could be supported by the existing fabric, which could only support its own weight. WilkinsonEyre worked closely with engineers, Buro Happold, to create a completely independent structure involving a complex jigsaw of beams and columns which rests partly on the existing concrete foundations with careful new foundations added in places between existing ones.

The retail units are housed in a series of new volumes positioned at Ground level inside the main colonnades in Turbine Halls A and B. The front portion of the roofs to these units acts a continuous walkway at Upper Ground running north to south.

Respecting the building's Grade II* Listing, WilkinsonEyre designed all shop fronts and brand signage, employing a vocabulary which responds to the original architecture: The expression of the shop fronts respects the layering of the original so that they maintain an important but subsidiary role in the overall composition. At Upper Ground and First Floor levels, the shop fronts have been designed as a set of metal portals sitting between the existing listed faience clad columns, with frameless glazing panels inside. This specific detail allows for future amendments to shopfronts without any need to interface with the historic listed fabric.

The Grade II* Listing prescribed a simple visual language in the building, including all branding. As such, WilkinsonEyre's brand guidelines for the individual shop units include details such as uniform monochrome dropdown signage above each retailer's door in order to maintain consistency throughout the retail areas. Each retailer is also encouraged to develop a bespoke fit-out for their Battersea shop rather than apply their usual kit of parts.

57

PARIS BAGUETTE
PARIS
BAGUETTE
ME+EM
CHANEL
PINKO
A.P.C.
REISS
RALPH LAUREN
GANT
LACOSTE

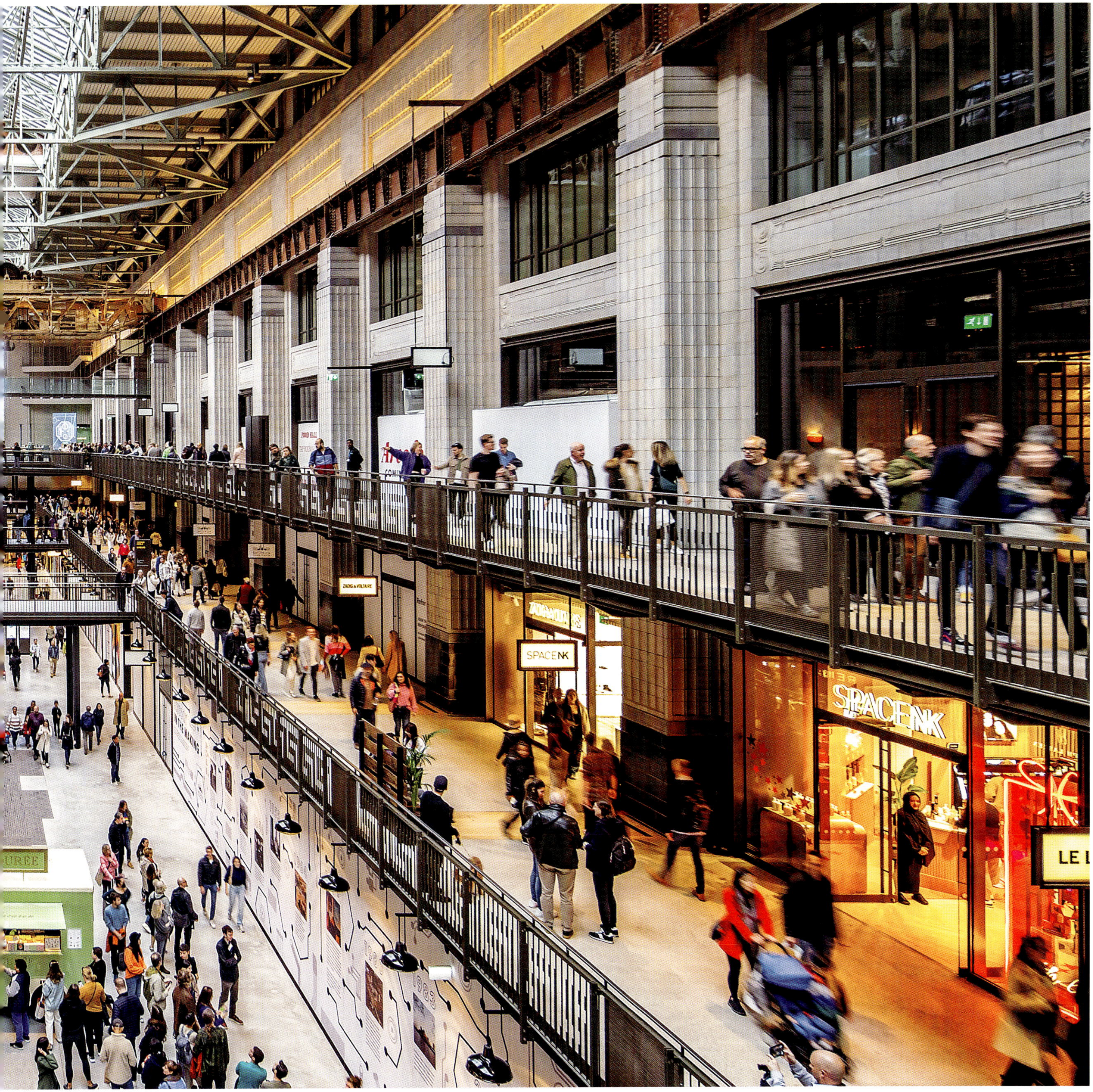
ZADIG & VOLTAIRE
SPACE NK
SPACE NK
LE L
URÉE

Turbine Hall A

Equal in size to the turbine hall at the Tate Modern, many of the original finishes and features of the existing 1930s 'Turbine Hall A' survived its 40-year neglect. Wherever possible, these features are incorporated into WilkinsonEyre's new design.

The Turbine Halls have been extensively restored: covered in asbestos, this work began with their complete decontamination. The faience tile cladding to the walls has been pinned throughout to ensure each tile remains securely fixed. In addition, the existing roof trusses have been discreetly reinforced to support a new roof garden above with heavier loading for planting and trees.

Among the new walkways and bridges, an existing gantry beam designed to carry massive loads in the Power Station is employed to suspend a new lightweight bridge linking a new events space to 'Control Room A.' A set of angled cables support the bridge which, in order to link the two misaligned spaces, is diagonal in plan. This design principle avoided the need to create new support columns or foundations.

As a former industrial building, the Power Station enjoyed very little natural light. As such, the architects worked hard from the outset to, wherever possible, bring daylight into the Turbine Halls. One key move to achieve this was the reopening of the cathedral-like windows at both ends of the space, which had been bricked up during World War II.

The historic rooflight panels have also been replaced with double glazed units and opening panels to naturally ventilate the space and act as smoke extractors.

above Detailed view of the historic columns restored against the new retail signage

opposite View of the new shopfront portals

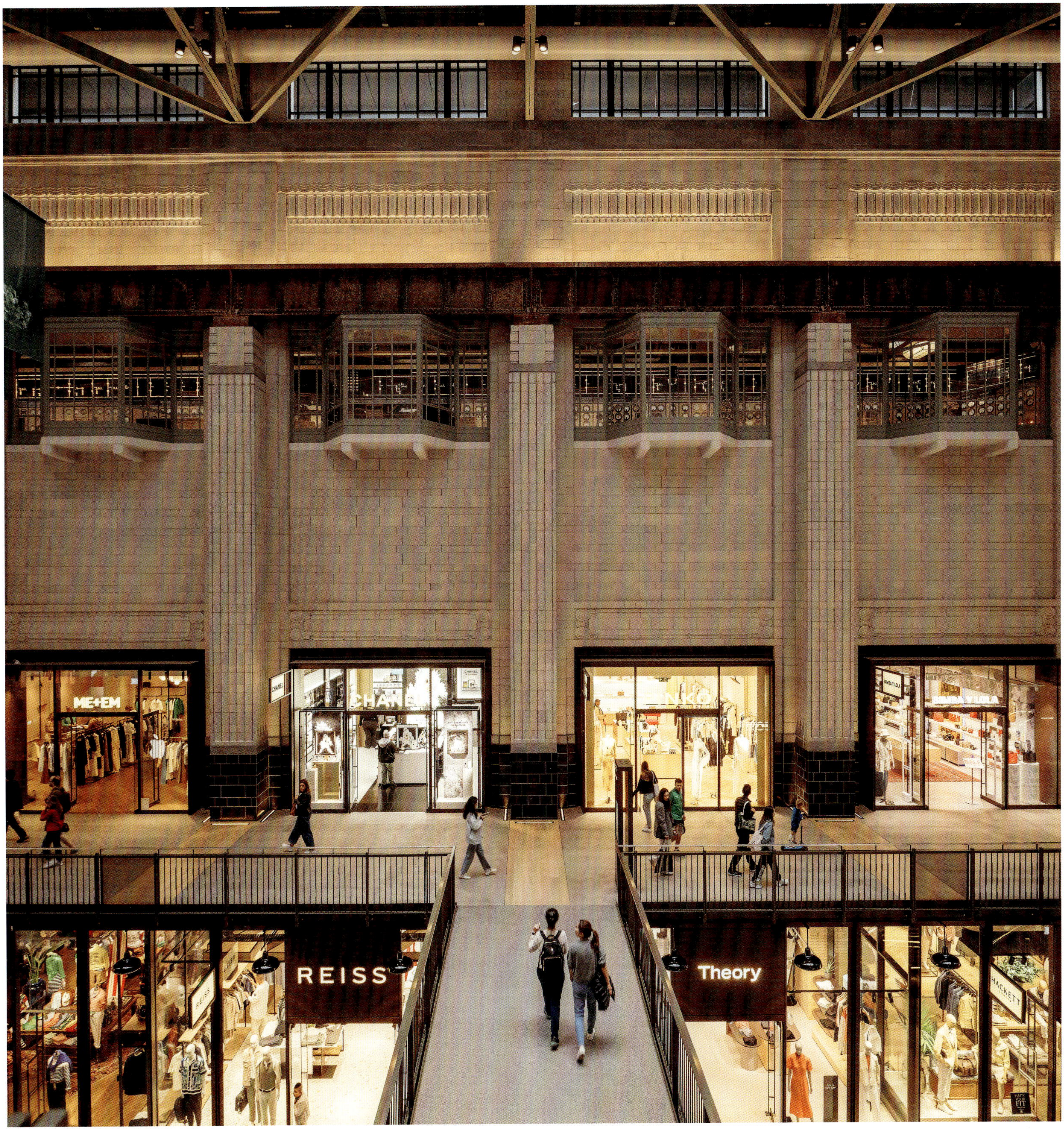
ME+EM
CHANEL
REISS
Theory
HACKETT

Control Room A

Perhaps the most recognisable space in the Power Station before its renovation, having been used as the backdrop to numerous movies and music videos, Control Room A is a spectacular Art Deco room that captures the essence of the Power Station's magic. The room was designed alongside Turbine Hall A in the 1930s, in the early life of domestic electricity, and was suitably glamorous and celebratory of this new technology.

The original control room for the entire Power Station, the room once sent power from Carnaby Street to Wimbledon, including Buckingham Palace and the Houses of Parliament. Those who worked within it were highly skilled and, as such, it incorporated the lavish and intricate finishes and detailing reserved for senior members of staff. Walls are covered in book-matched lunel rubane marble, framed with Belgian Black. The gold painted metal ceiling held translucent glass that flooded the room with daylight whilst the bay windows included an early form of double glazing to helped reduce the sound of the turbines. The floor is comprised of richly coloured teak herringbone parquet.

Unfortunately, the room was in an extreme state of disrepair when first surveyed by WilkinsonEyre in 2013; it required an in-depth restoration involving the painstaking repair or replacement of many dials and the replacement or decontamination of all glazing in the ceiling which, like much of the glazing across the Power Station, had been painted out during World War II to avoid visibility by the German Luftwaffe.

This space has now been restored to its original glory. It can be visited by the public but is also designed for use as a private event space for a limited number of guests.

above The historic windows restored

opposite Glazed ceiling and control panels restored back to their original glory

63

Turbine Hall B

Whilst the 1950s interior architecture in Turbine Hall B is very different to that of its earlier counterpart, WilkinsonEyre's light touch treatment in the space took a similar approach to that employed in Turbine Hall A, using walkways and horizontal bridges to break it up whilst maintaining its monumental qualities and glimpses to the existing fabric.

Elements of the original historic fabric are retained and subtly celebrated throughout. As in Turbine Hall A, the footprint of where the turbines used to sit is illustrated on the floor by a change in materials, while a former gantry crane is used to hang a feature 'band stand;' a giant glass moveable box used throughout the year to house various creative interventions including artworks or advertising stunts. An LED matrix allows projection onto the box itself.

The lack of natural light in Turbine Hall B was even more pronounced than in Turbine Hall A. To remedy this, the team developed a set of bespoke light tubes to bring light into the space from the roof garden above. These 2.5m deep cylinders are covered by glass in the rooftop park above and incorporate a reflective lining to bring light into the space. Highly effective during the day, at nighttime they are combined with an artificial lighting system.

Upon inspection, the Turbine Hall's original curved concrete roof tiles were found to be dangerous, due in part to their weight as well as to their rusted fixings. These have been replaced by glass reinforced concrete tiles, identical in form but much lighter and safer to dismount for inspection and maintenance.

adidas
ROX
ROX
BREITLING
BREITLING 1884
Abercrombie & Fitch
Levi's

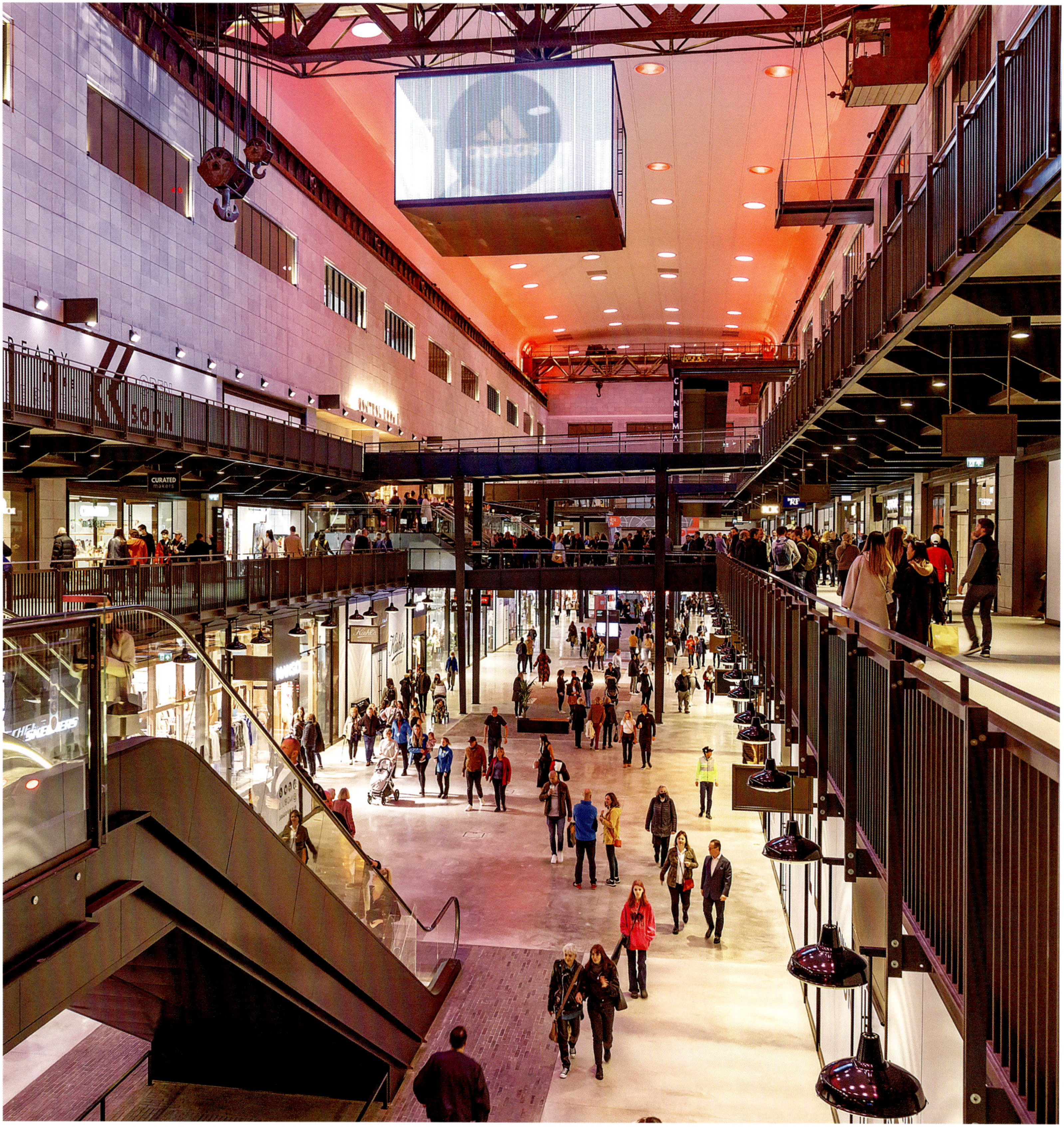
CURATED
makers
CINEMA

Bandstand suspended from the existing gantry crane

Control Room B

By the time that Control Room B was constructed between 1937 and 1941, the lavish finishes of Control Room A had given way to the more utilitarian materials appropriate to war time. The stainless steel control desk and freestanding synchroscopes to the front controlled the 66 kV output of the Power Station to match the standards of the national grid. As with Control Room A, the room has been painstakingly decontaminated, repaired and polished, involving extensive research and delicate specialized work.

The room was always an integral part of Turbine Hall B and Wilkinson Eyre decided that within the new retail environment, the room should remain the active focal point. They have created an opportunity for people to engage with the history of the Power Station in an every day way, introducing a cocktail bar in the space, discretely separated from the control panels by a curved low level glass wall, so that the public might enjoy a drink whilst sitting amongst the original dials and controls.

CONTROL ROOM B

below Control Room B restored pre retail fit-out

opposite New retail interiors engaging with control room panels

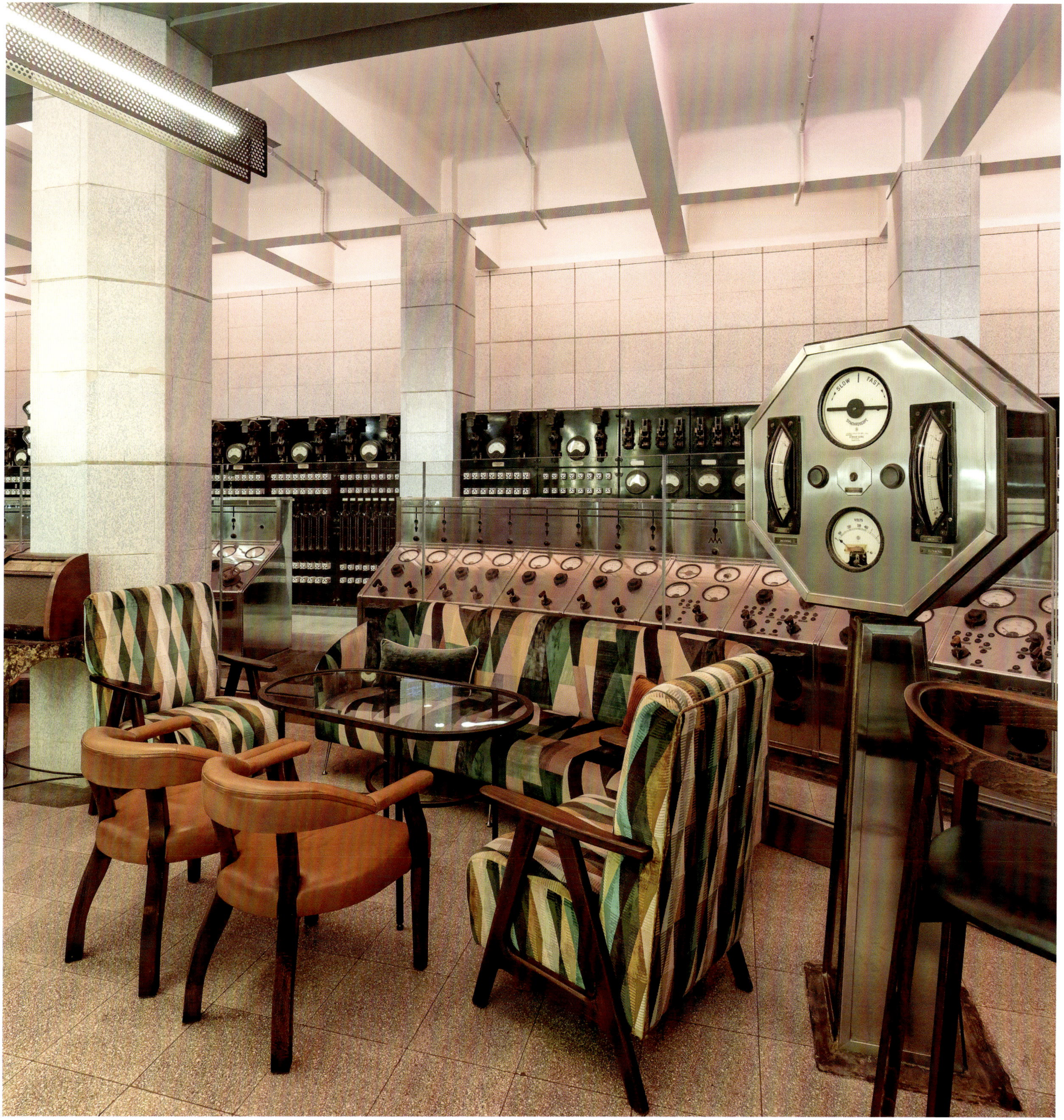
SLOW
FAST
VOLTS

North and South Entrances

Two atriums at each end of the Boiler House mark the main public entrances to the building. The South Atrium is the main entrance for the majority of visitors coming from the new tube station. Designed as a full height atrium, its glass roof gives views of the chimney. To keep as much of the historic façade visible as possible here, very little restoration has been done. The scars from its years of use as an industrial building and subsequent years of neglect remain visible, a feat achieved using a minimal bow string steelwork structure to hold the façade in place.

A similar approach is taken in the North Atrium where the exposed historic façade has had limited restoration and reveals some previously demolished elements such as the original staff staircase. New interventions in the space, including a series of link bridges, have been stepped away from the historic façade, allowing uninterrupted views of the original brick wall as the well newly replaced steel-framed windows. Directly accessible from North Park, this atrium also acts as the main entry point to the event space at Level One, accessed via a feature staircase or a set of monumental lateral escalators.

Original competition sketch

Superimposition of the existing façade

Illustrative rendering of the proposed atrium wall support

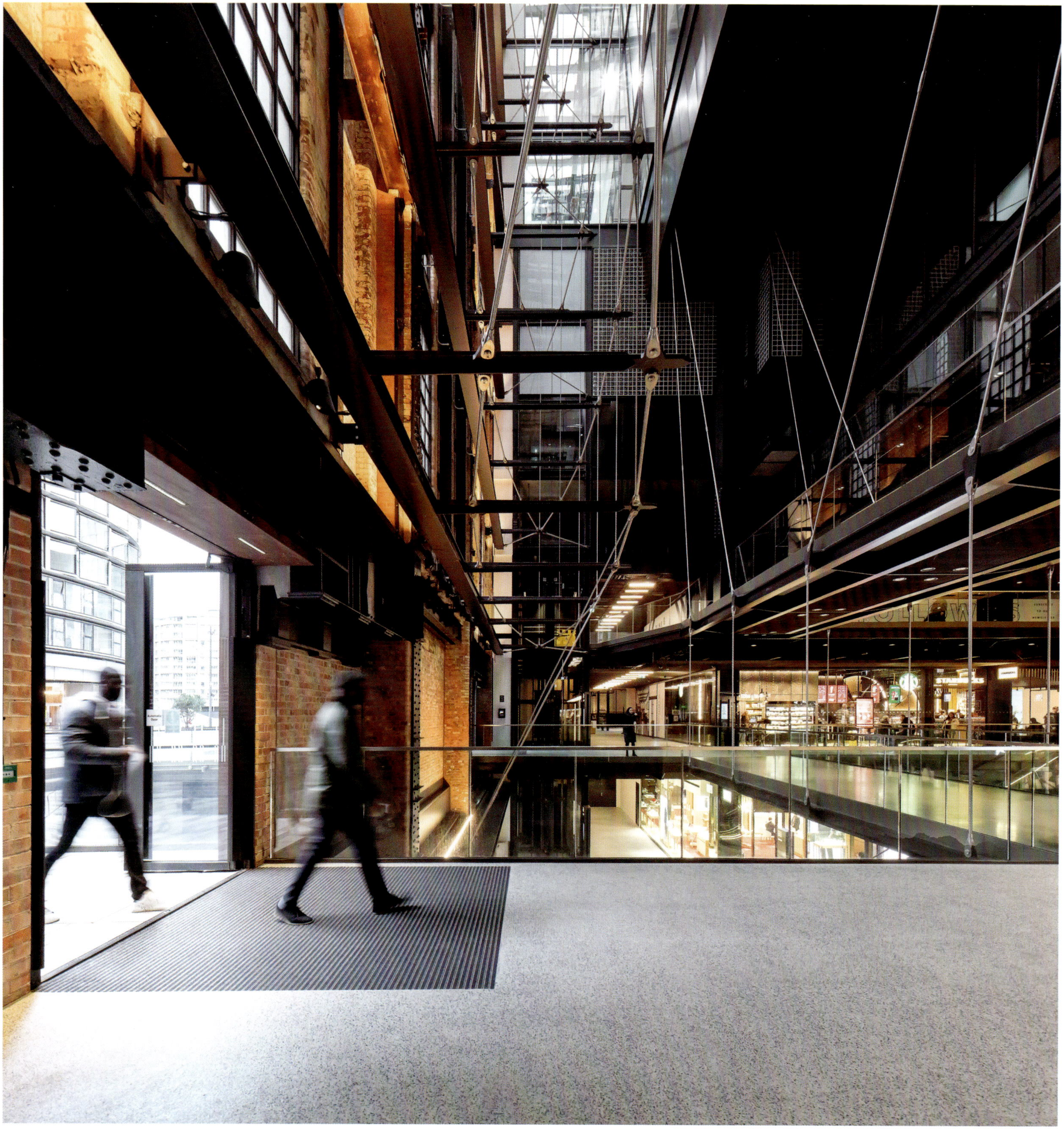

left South Entrance

right View looking up at North Entrance

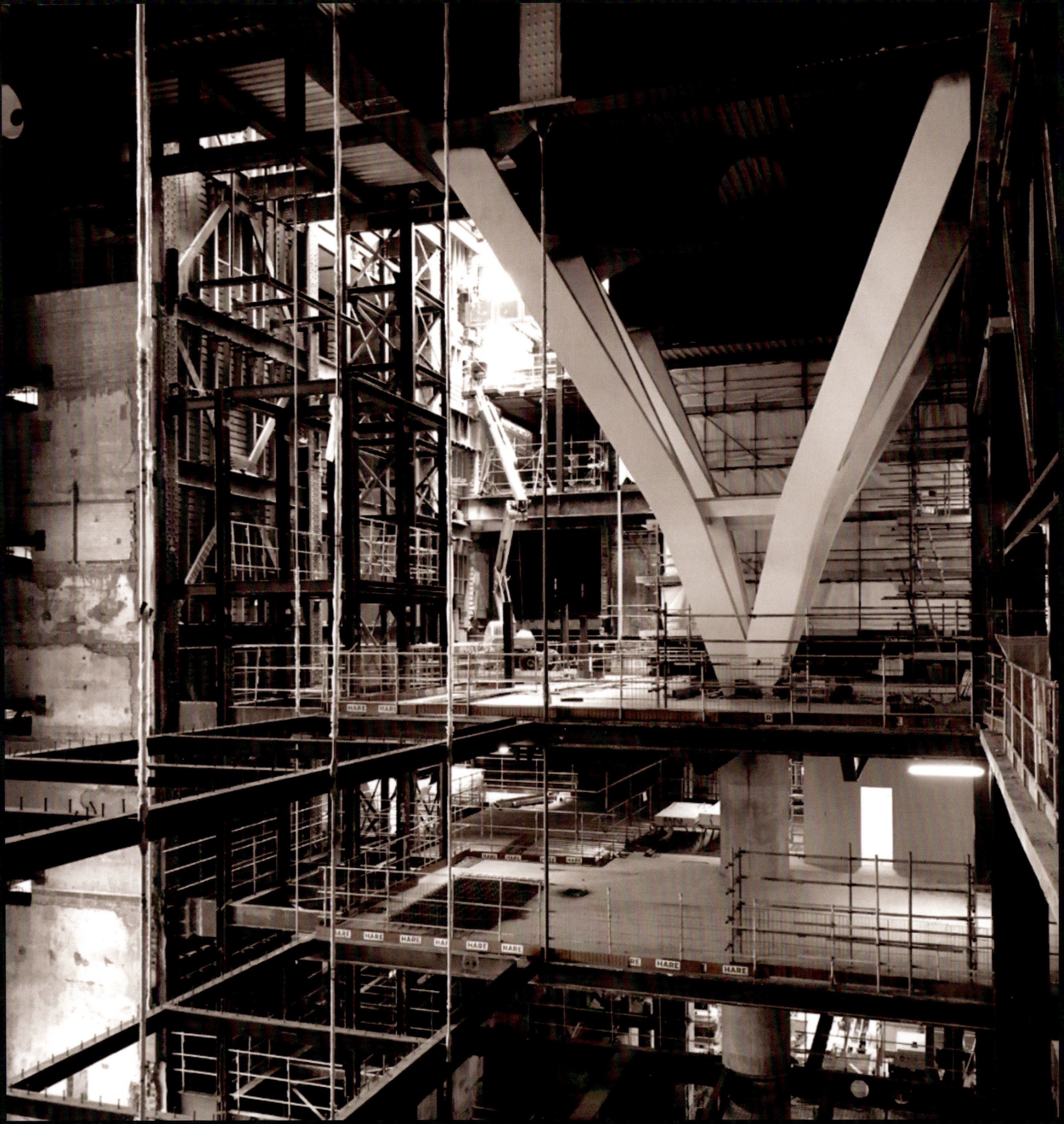
HARE

Events

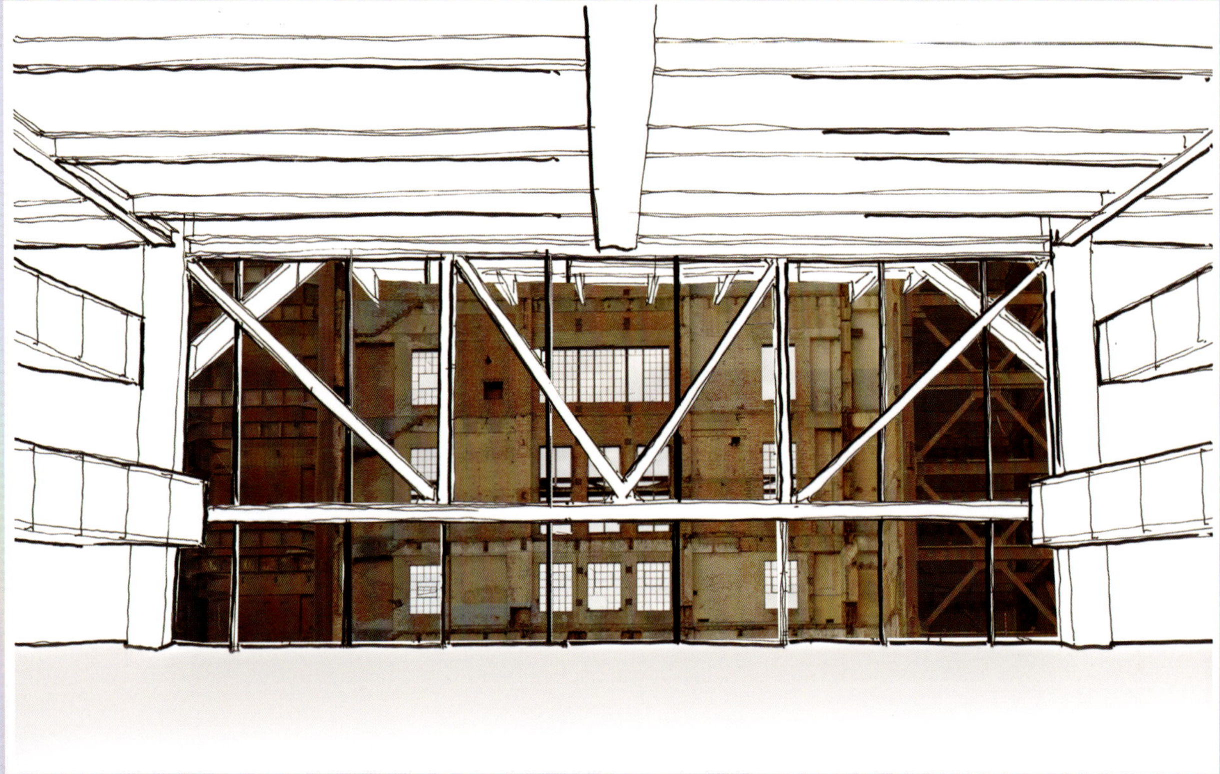

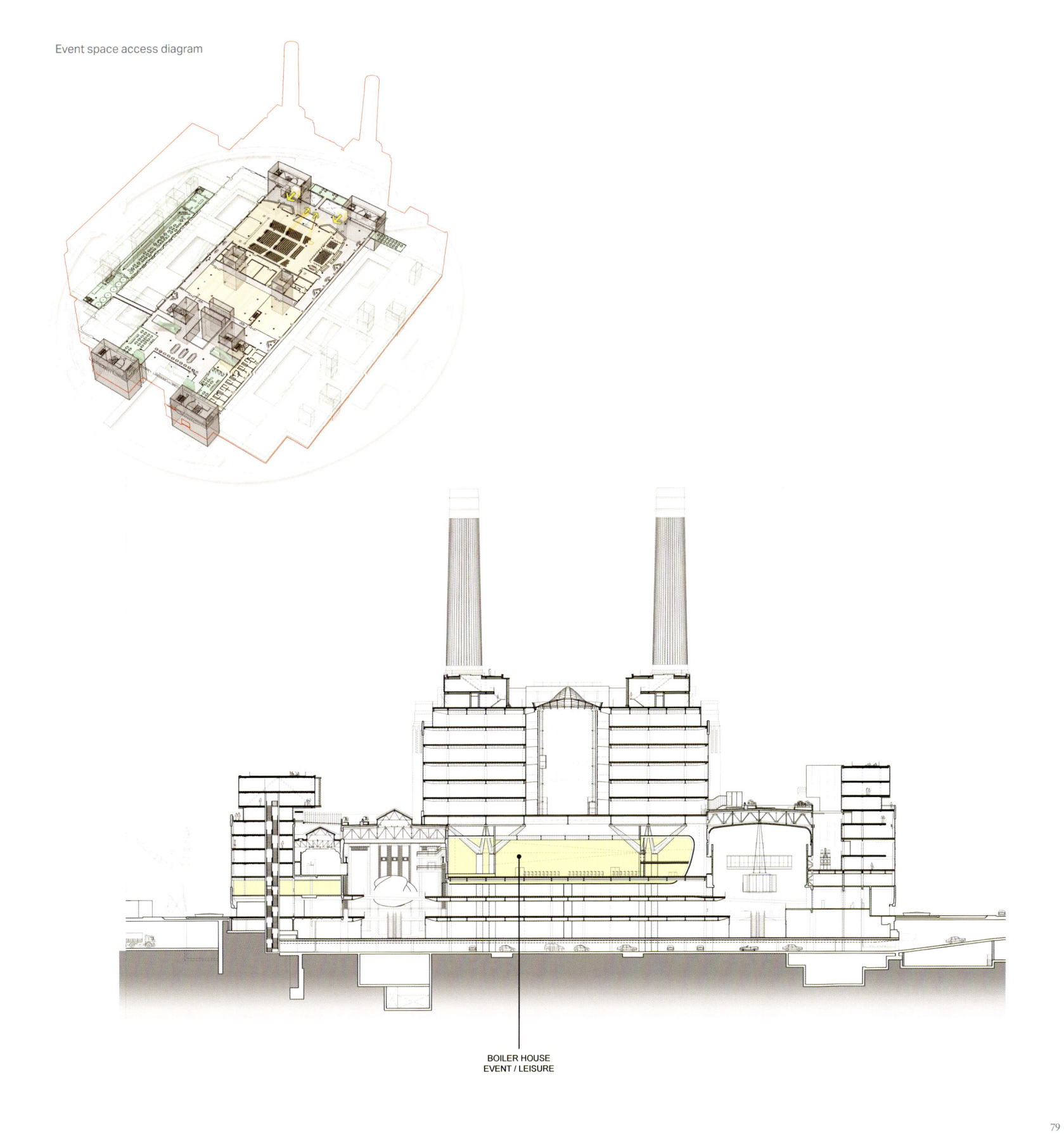

Event space access diagram

BOILER HOUSE
EVENT / LEISURE

Adding to the multi-functional programme in the building, a state-of-the-art event space has been created on Level Two of the Boiler House, directly accessible from the North Entrance. Originally designed to accommodate a variety of events, with a standing capacity of 2000, this three-storey height volume has been conceived as a column-free space, avoiding any obstruction between spectator and artist. The space spans above the retail area and below six stories of office and two levels of residential above.

The column-free space was achieved by creating a transfer structure which converts the single support columns in the retail spaces below to six columns in the office area above. WilkinsonEyre achieved this feat through a pair of 'structural trees': triple height sculptural columns whose single column base splays like a tree to transfer its load across six columns above.

As per the general design philosophy for the project, a visual relationship is maintained between the Event Space and the building's historic fabric by integrating a giant window to the north into the North Atrium. This window employs a bespoke high acoustic performance glazing system: a set of double glazed units on one side of a mega truss with a single glazed panel to the other side. Additional acrylic moveable panels are installed to absorb sound from the event box itself.

opposite Cut perspective view of the event space with retail below and office above

left View of the feature staircase in the North Atrium

MITCHELLSON
MITCHELLSON
MITCHELLSON
MITCHELLSON
MITCHELLSON
Select

Residential

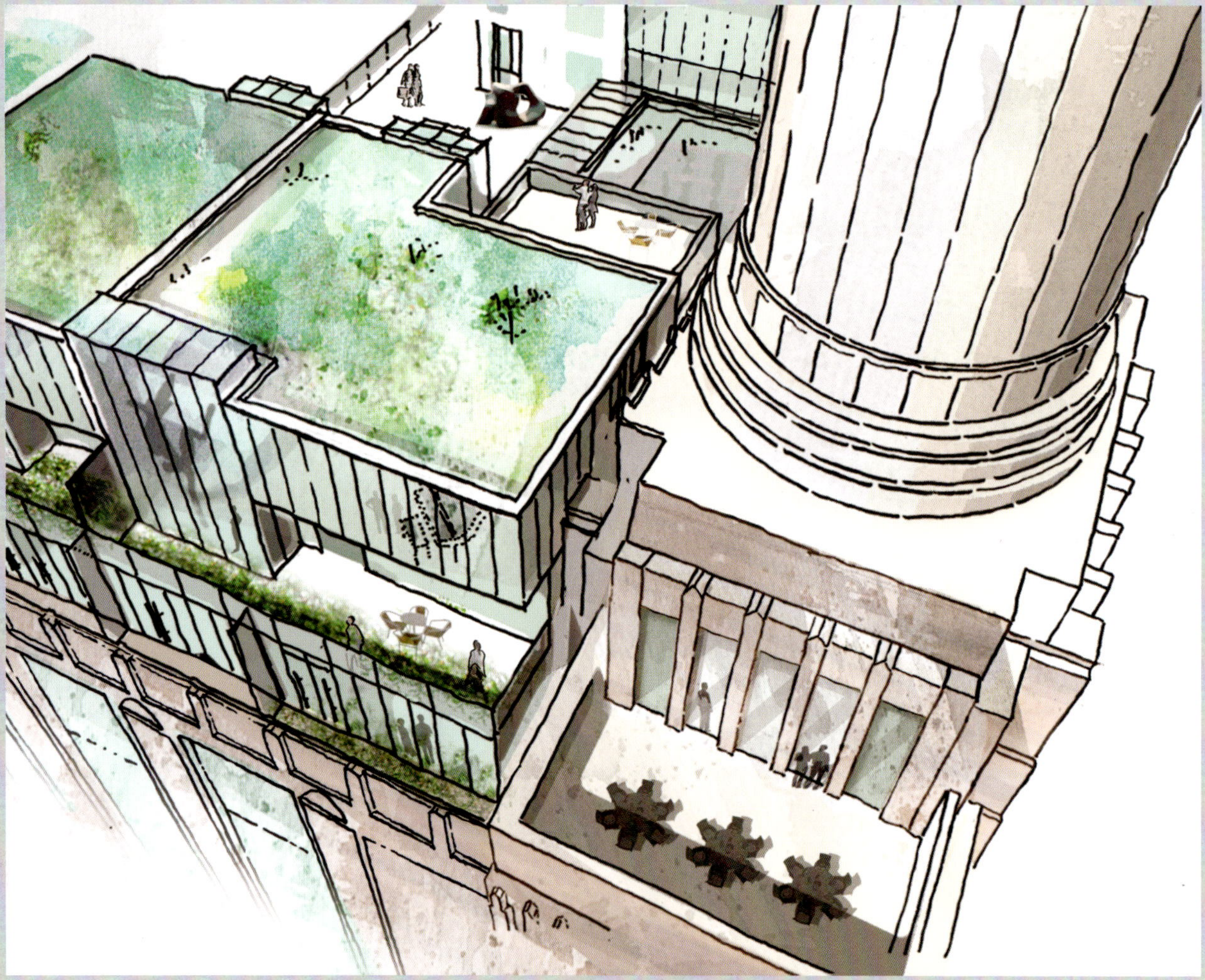

Residential Access Diagram

Boiler House Square

Switch House West

Switch House East

Switch House West | Turbine Hall A | Boiler House | Turbine Hall B | Switch House East

85

A Mixed-Use Scheme

The Power Station project originally started as a residential-led masterplan. The brief later shifted to create a mixed-use scheme which could be open to the public. A significant amount of housing was, however, retained in the plan and located in the lateral volumes of the Power Station (partially in the existing building and partially in new build additions). 'Switch House West and East' are thinner volumes and, as such, more appropriate spaces within which to create residential properties. Their linear elevation also lent itself to being altered to provide the natural light necessary for homes.

WilkinsonEyre designed the main architecture of the residential spaces including the external envelope and all communal areas. Michaelis Boyd were appointed to create a concept for the internal look and feel of the apartments which WilkinsonEyre were responsible for rolling out.

Boiler House Apartments

The 75m X 150m roof of the Boiler House volume - the main volume between the four chimneys - offered WilkinsonEyre an exciting opportunity to create a completely private world for residents in the centre of London, directly at the base of the chimneys. A series of single storey apartments have been built to the lower level with incredible open views towards central London. In addition, a series of L-shaped duplex villas, each in the region of 250 sqm, offer double-aspect living. These villas all benefit from their own roof gardens, balconies and garden at grade.

As with the Switch House apartments, the outward facing façades of these apartments are in slick glass, while those facing into the roof gardens have individual stone portals to temper the scale of the space. They deliver a completely unique living experience – a secluded terrace of houses at the base of the Power Station's historic chimneys.

The Boiler House Apartments enjoy a spectacular entrance experience: at the four corners of the Power Station, residents enter through the wash towers' weathering steel portals. Adorned with modern stained-glass panels, these each offer access to a pair of wall-climbing glass lifts which ascend through a 21m height atrium. Each lift then travels six storeys in an enclosed shaft (through the office spaces), before emerging into a magnificent glass ceilinged lobby offering views up through it towards the sly.

Contrasting marble has been inserted to the exposed concrete inner walls of the chimney.

The villas here are designed as a modern interpretation of the Georgian or Victorian garden square, albeit on top of Battersea Power Station, a hidden residential haven.

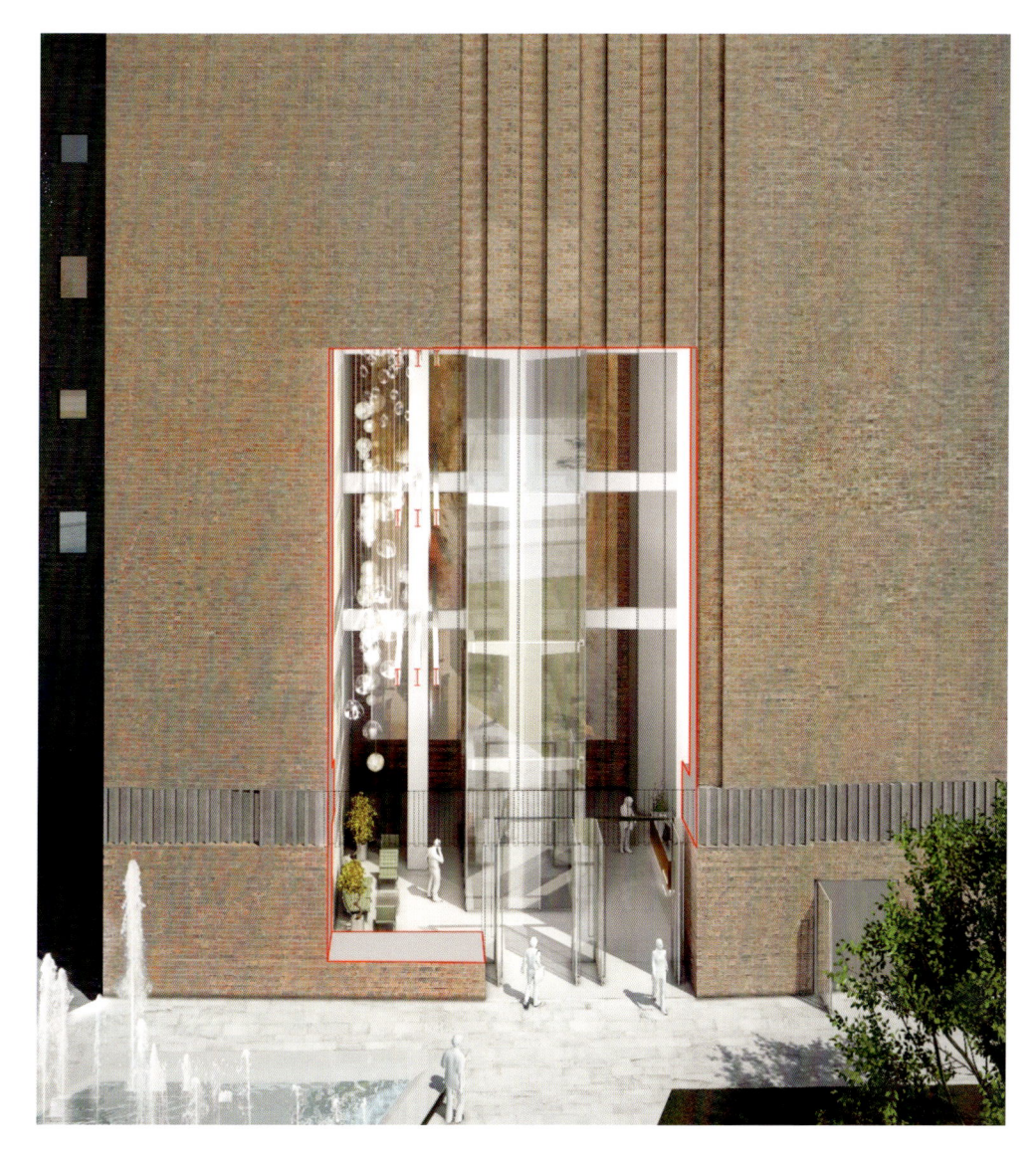

above Cut-out rendering of the Boiler House residential lobby

right Cut-out rendering of the Boiler House residential sky lobby

above Light fittings designed by Speirs Major

below Sky Lobby, where strips of marble have been inserted into the exposed concrete of the chimney's interior

right Detail of the wall climber lift

Boiler House entrance lobby

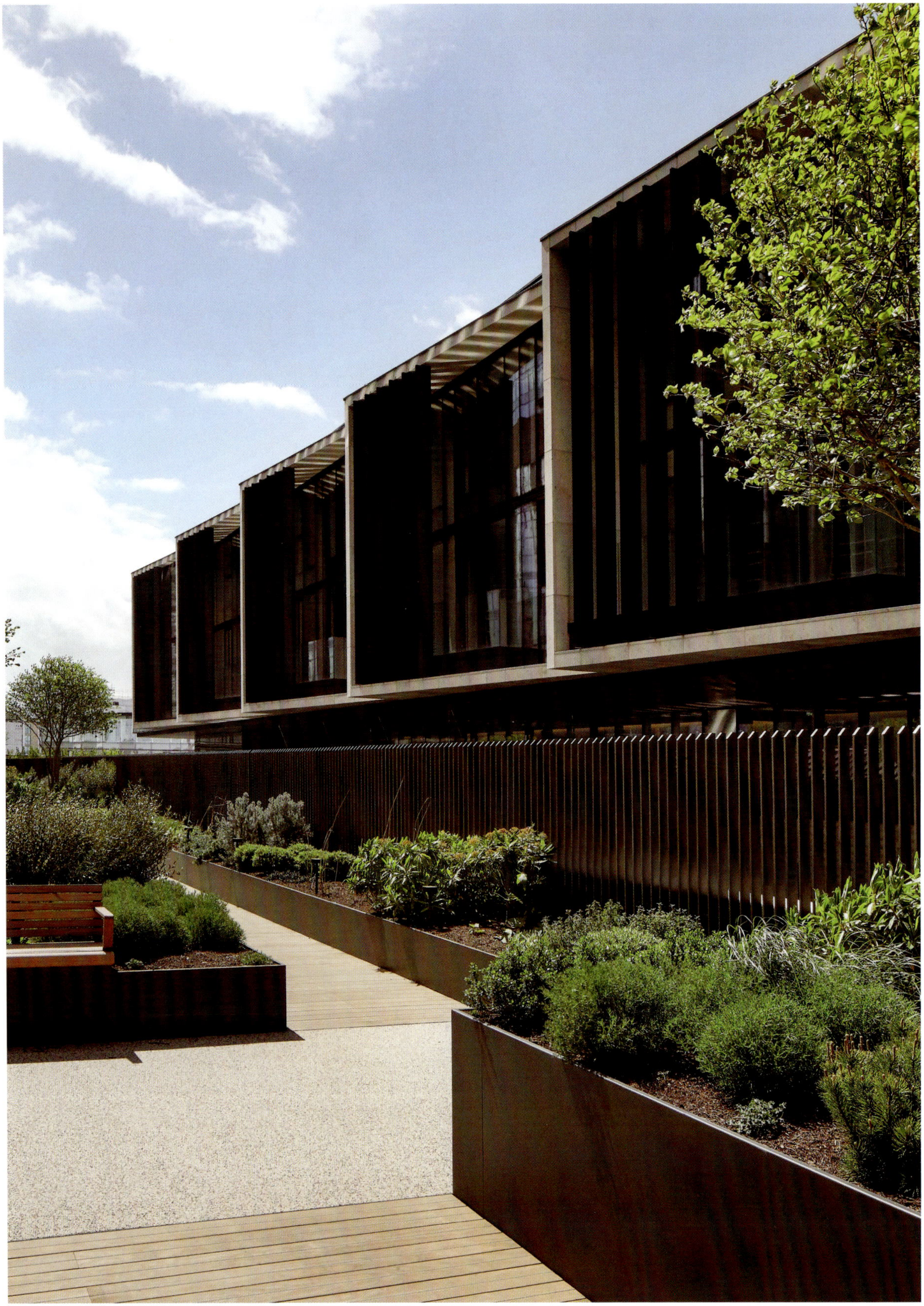

Turbine Hall A residential communal garden

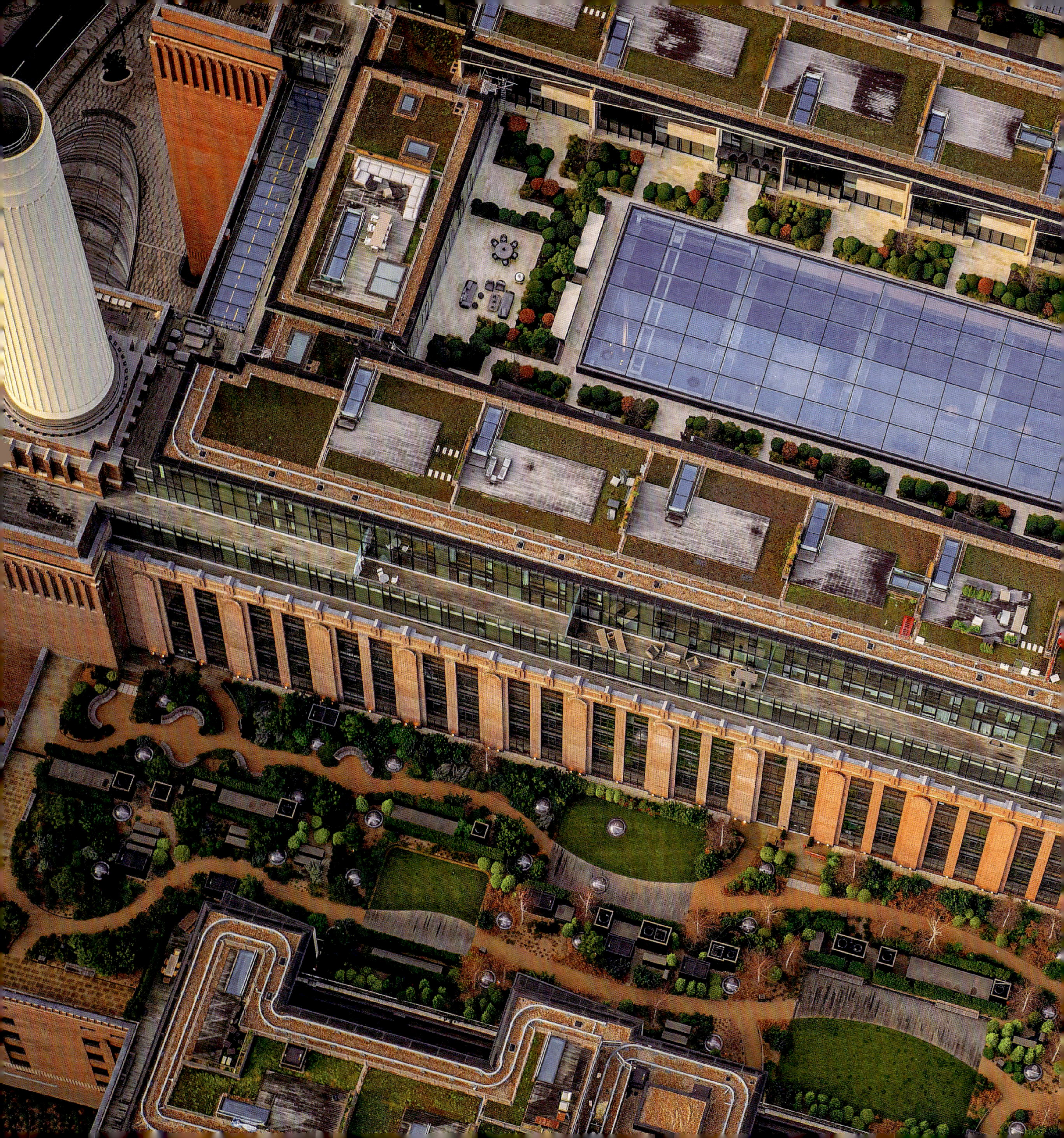

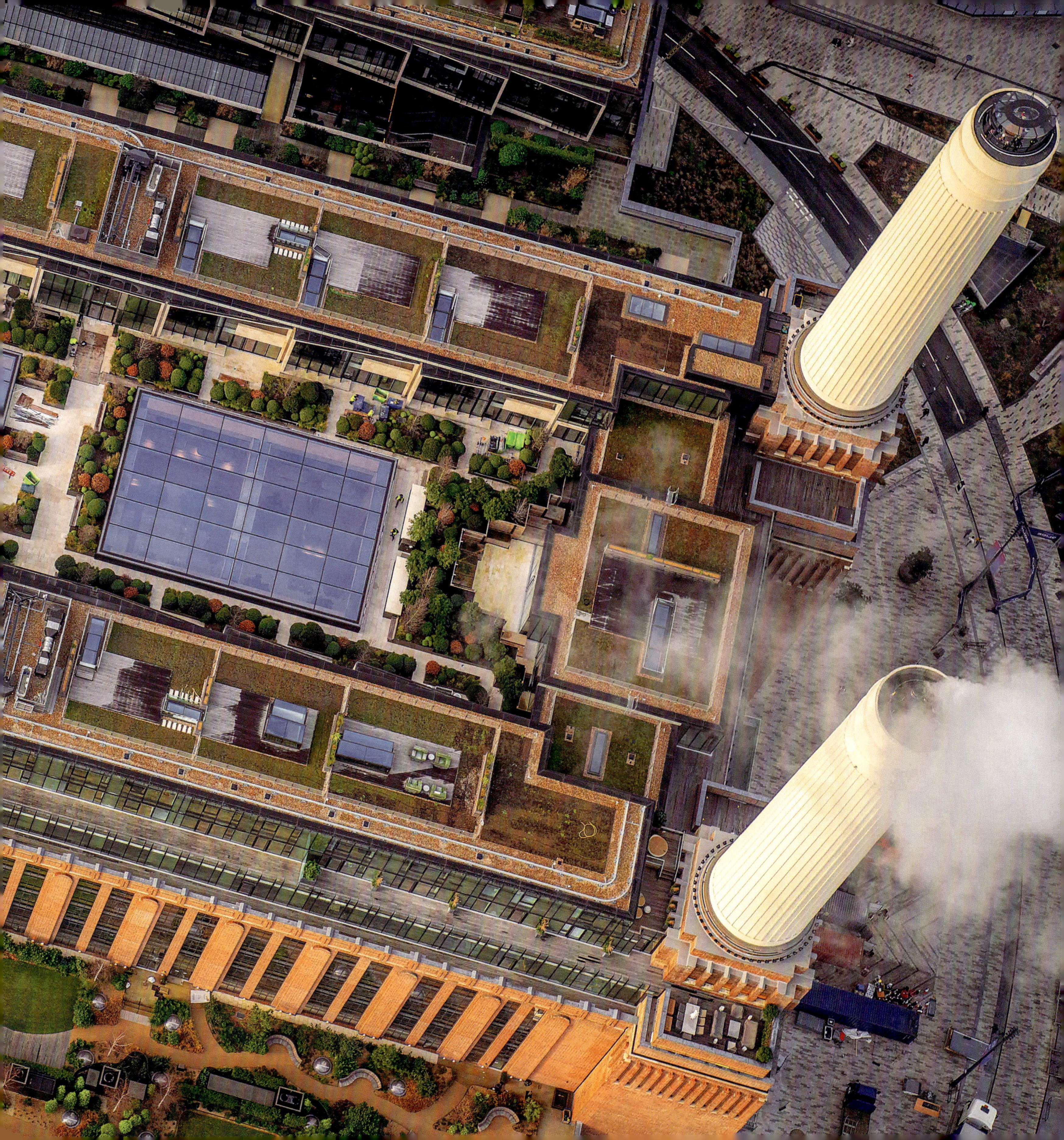

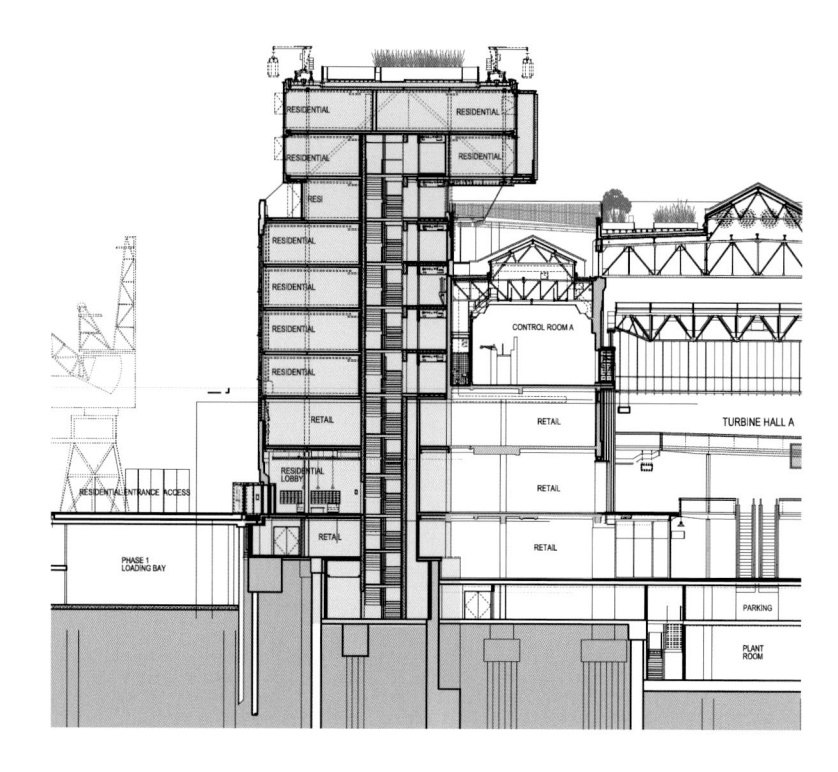

Switch House West

Switch House West is home to 92 residential units, housed in five storeys of the existing building topped by a three-storey extension. Once home to the Power Station's main switch gear, laboratory, battery and assembly rooms; the original slab had been demolished during the 1980s, when a developer had introduced a steel frame into the building in preparation for what was ultimately an abortive scheme. This frame was already damaged, not original and not fit for its new purpose. The majority of it was therefore removed leaving only the original Power Station walls to be retained along with the existing volume of Control Room A.

The residential components of the Power Station required, more than any other part of the building, a sensitivity to scale and a thoughtful approach to tempering its vast spaces in order to make them more human. At a length of 120m, the Switch Houses posed significant challenge in this respect. WilkinsonEyre's solution was to carve out internal courtyards, reducing the depths of the floorplans to a more liveable 7m, whilst also offering the properties, where possible, double-aspect rooms.

Control Room A, with its glazed roof, sits in the middle of Switch House West. To avoid blocking light, the top two floors of the Switch House's new extension cantilever over the top of it using a clever cross-braced structure designed by engineers Buro Happold. In addition to the shared rooftop courtyard spaces, each apartment in the three-storey extension enjoys its own outdoor space. To achieve this, the first level of extension steps back to create a 2.5m terrace. Above this, the duplex apartments cantilever back out again, whilst enjoying their own individual roof terrace.

As with other new interventions to the Power Station, the apartment blocks are created a as a floating glass volume above the listed brick wall. This design creates an elegant extension which respects the simplicity of the existing volume below, the glass aspect of the façade complementing the brick wall without competing with it. Facing onto the shared roof garden, a series of stone 'portals' subdivide the apartments' 120m long shared façade. Angled for privacy, the portals give the effect of a terrace of houses, offering front doors and human scale.

The main access to the apartments is through a three-storey height atrium to the back of Control Room A's brick wall. Walkways cantilever out into this space, creating a dramatic entrance sequence. Oversized doors with side panels have been thoughtfully designed to lend an individual quality to each home. This is achieved using careful detailing, including a change in flooring and ceiling finishes, differentiated balustrade detailing and bespoke ironmongery to mark the threshold to each apartment.

The material palette here, again, responds to the historic fabric of the Power Station whilst creating a warm and modern feel across the residential units. A portion of the historic external brick wall is left exposed in each apartment, while huge full height slot windows have been cut out of the historic fabric to bring natural light into all apartments.

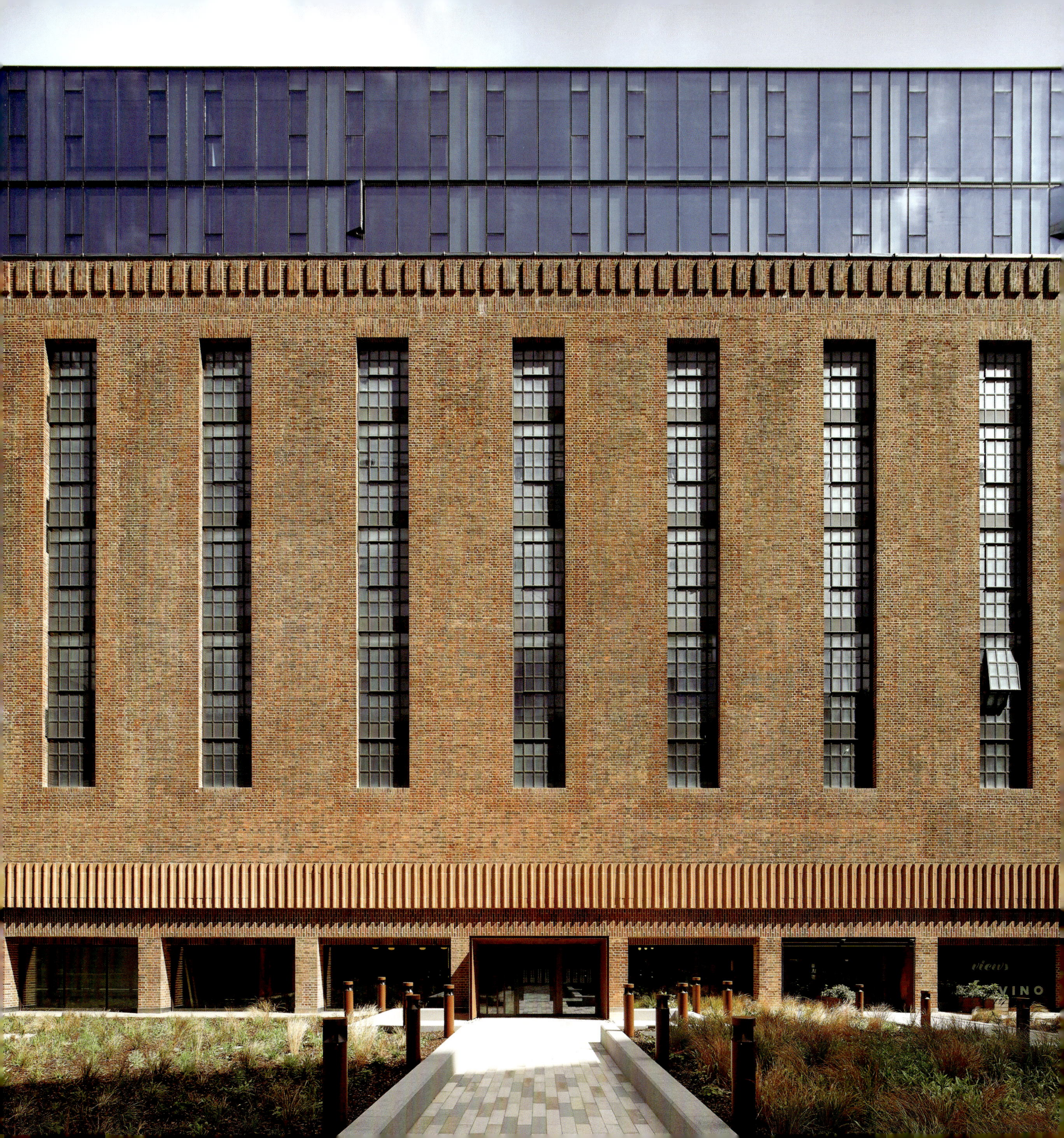
VINO

above Switch House West residential lobby

below Switch House West residential corridor

above Switch House West living room with exposed historic brickwork

below Switch House West duplex entrance view

Switch House East

The 105 apartments in Switch House East take on a similar typology to their counterparts in Switch House West, albeit with a more industrial feel. The warm palette of 1930s inspired materials in West – bronze, dark wood, colourful tiles to all communal areas – is substituted for a cooler palette of blonde woods, weathered steel and exposed concrete, with services left either exposed or veiled with steel mesh.

A double-height lobby space has been created against the wall of Control Room B, which incorporates fun details and references to the historic Power Station. A heavily rivetted stanchion beam has been salvaged from the existing building, where it used to support one of the chimneys: here it is used to create a reception desk, above which original lights have been rewired and fitted. Equipment from the Power Station is also used sculpturally in one of the courtyards, enlivening the spaces and firmly locating the apartments in their historic setting.

The Switch House East apartments share a communal outdoor space on the roof of Turbine Hall B. These gardens are shared with the offices opposite them, physically separated by subtle planting and trellises.

Several one-off residential properties are located within the original fabric of the north and south elevations of the Power Station, each with a unique spatial arrangement prescribed by the existing building geometry. One such property within the north elevation enjoys a monumental two storey square window, positioned in the void left by the original coal chute. When the building functioned as a Power Station, this was the opening where coal would have been delivered into the internal turbines via conveyor belt from the riverside jetty.

The residential properties in Switch House East and West are a unique residential offer, creating refined warm modern living accommodation which contrasts beautifully with the exposed industrial heritage.

SWITCH
HOUSE
EAST
1–60
SWITCH
HOUSE
EAST
1–60
WITCH
IOUSE
AST
61–119

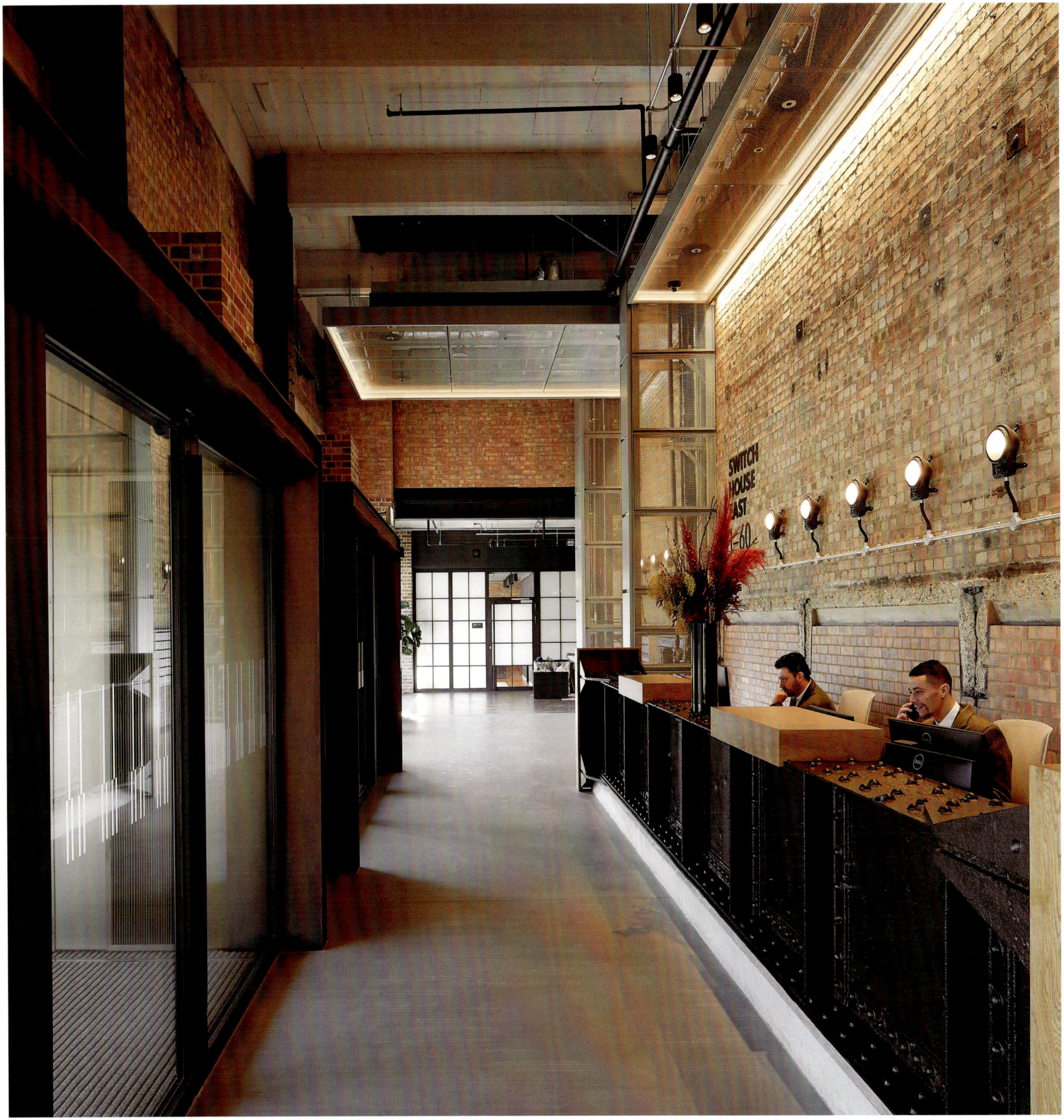
SWITCH
HOUSE

opposite Switch House East entrance lobby

above Switch House East detail view of entrance lobby

right Switch House East sunken courtyard

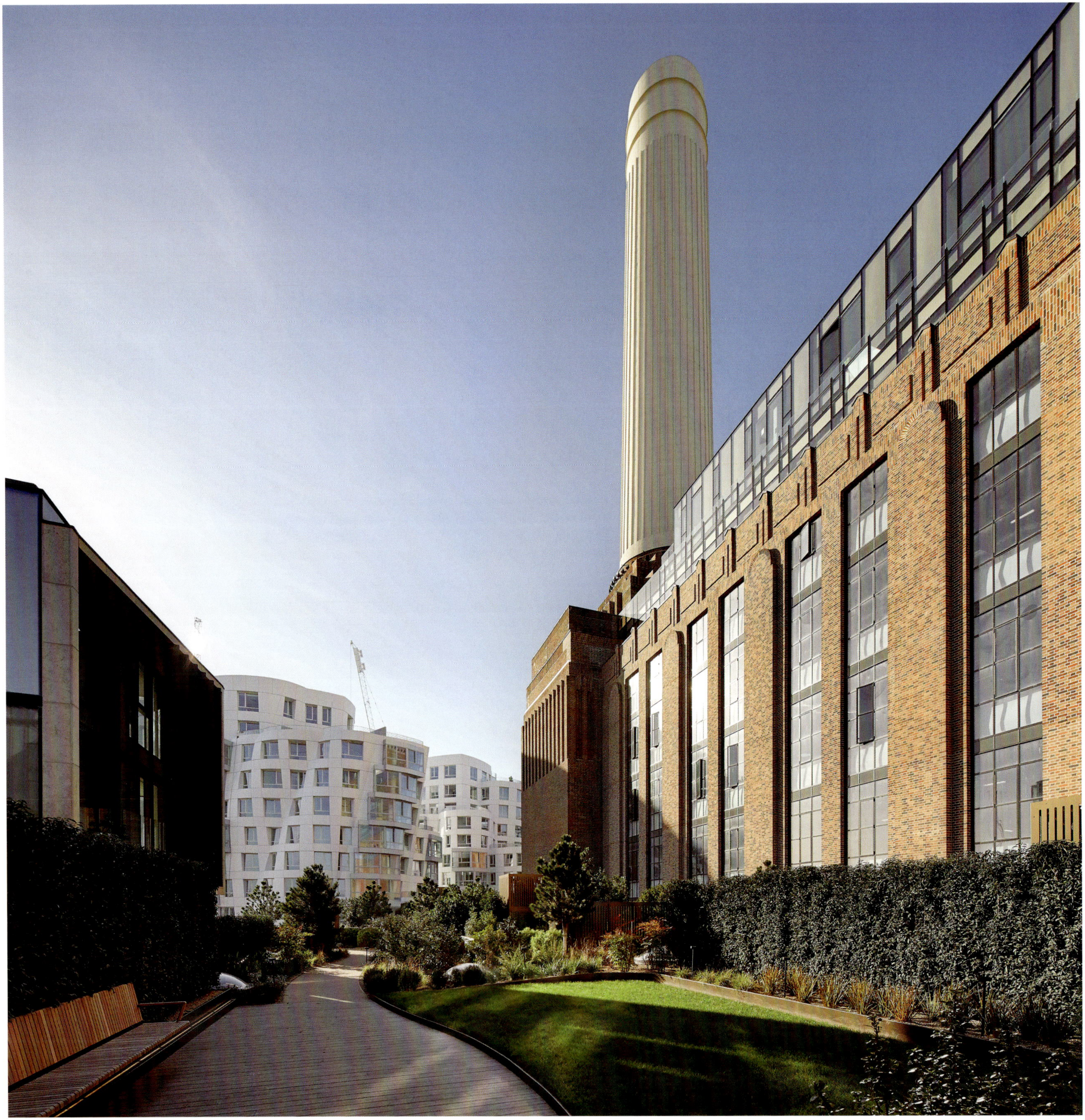

Turbine Hall B communal residential and office garden

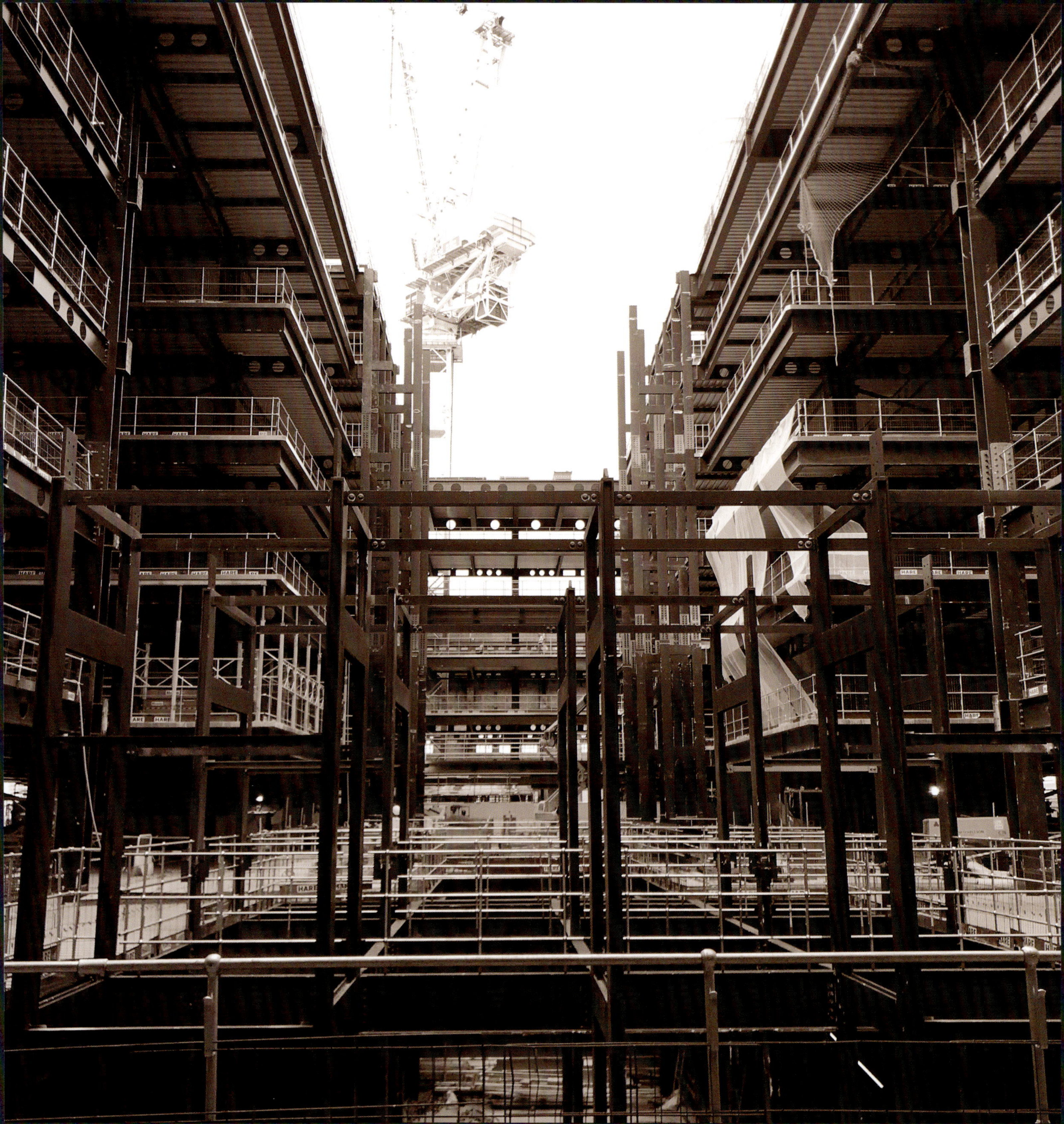

Offices

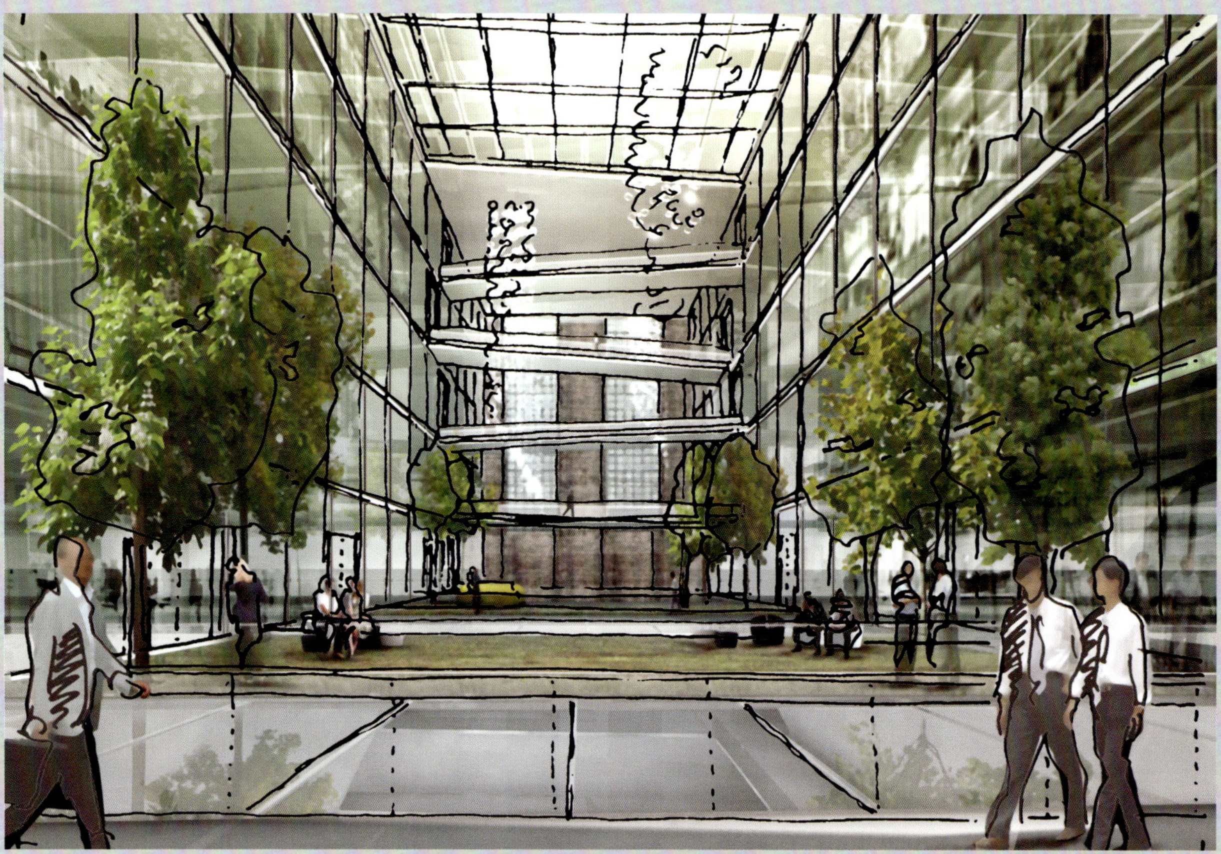

Office Access Diagram

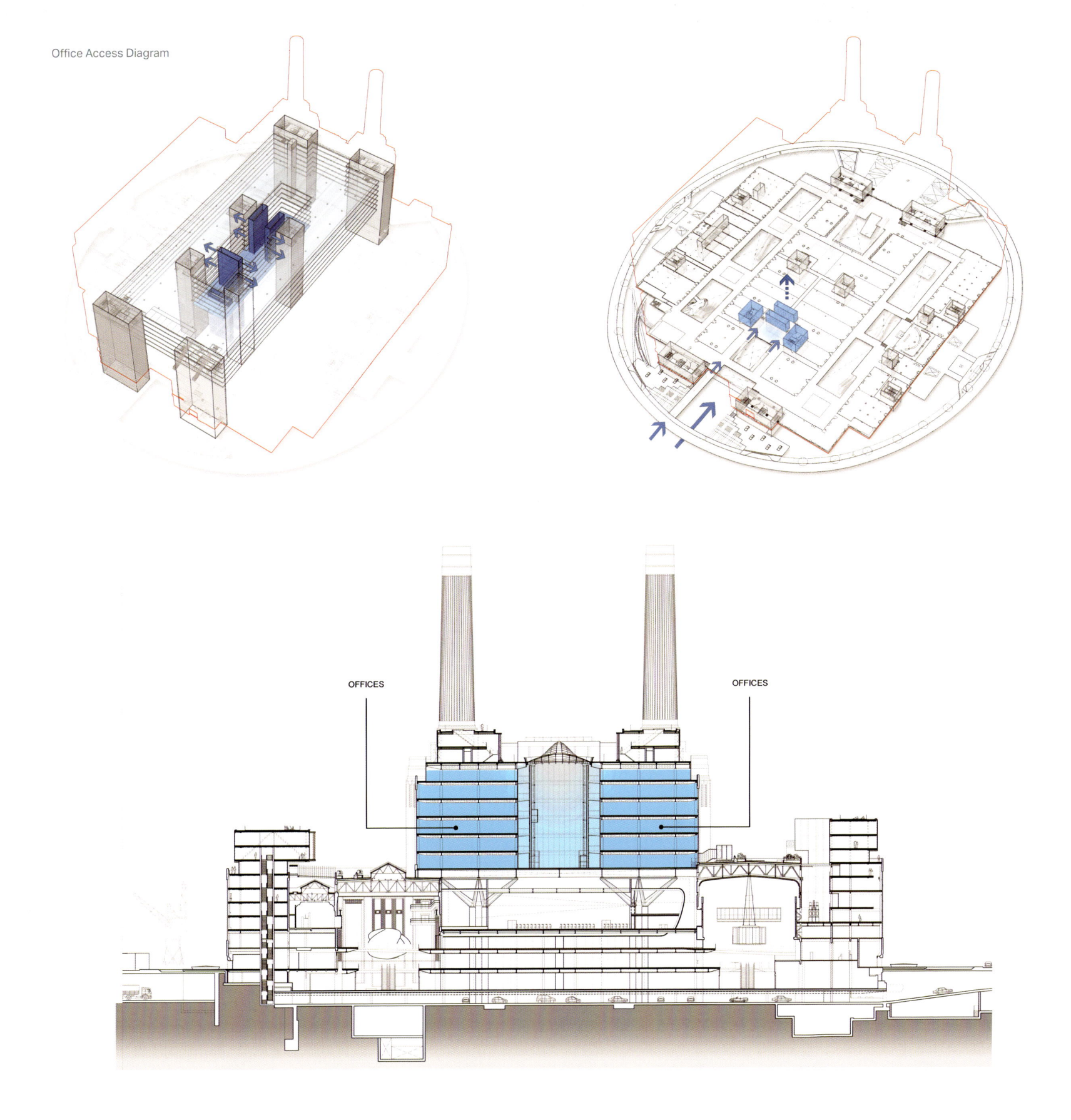

OFFICES

OFFICES

above Typical office floor plan

opposite Office entrance lobby

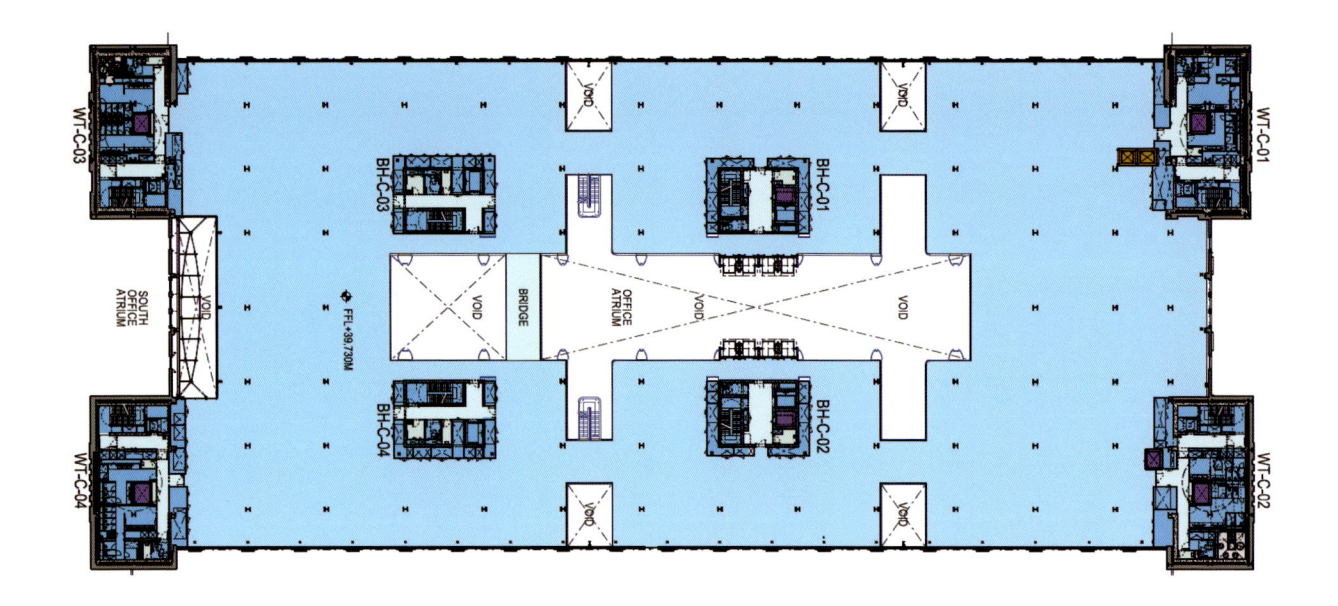

Before the Power Station redevelopment project, Battersea was not generally considered an office quarter in London. Part of the Section 106 Agreement for the project, however, included the extension of the Northern Line to the area; the connectivity offered by a new tube station suddenly made commercial development a viable and attractive possibility. And when Apple chose the Power Station as the location for its new London Headquarters, this possibility was cemented. WilkinsonEyre designed the shell and core, and communal areas for the office element, while Apple's fitout was undertaken by architects Foster + Partners.

The listed building was not ideally suited to the provision of Grade A office space. Its deep floorplan, with 7500 sqm floorplates, limited opportunity for natural light. Taking inspiration from the 'studio-style' offices popular among London's creative industries, WilkinsonEyre capitalised on the industrial heritage of the Power Station to provide a unique office environment.

When the Power Station was surveyed in the early 2000s, the west wall of the Boiler House had already collapsed, while the east wall was found to be structurally unsafe. As such, both needed replacing, offering the opportunity to introduce light into the space: window slots were introduced into the east and west elevations, with two tall openable windows installed in each bay, responding to the vertical motif of the original architecture.

At around 45,000 sqm, the office component of the Power Station is equivalent in scale to the 'Gherkin.' Entered directly from the retail space, it follows the Asian model with a modest 250 sqm lobby at ground floor and a much larger sky lobby at Level Five. Accessed via eight spectacular wall-climbing lifts, the 80 x 20m atrium has a fully glazed roof, flooding light into the formerly dark space. At six stories high, with 22m width between the office spaces, the atrium is the scale of a London street. Vents on either side bring in fresh air.

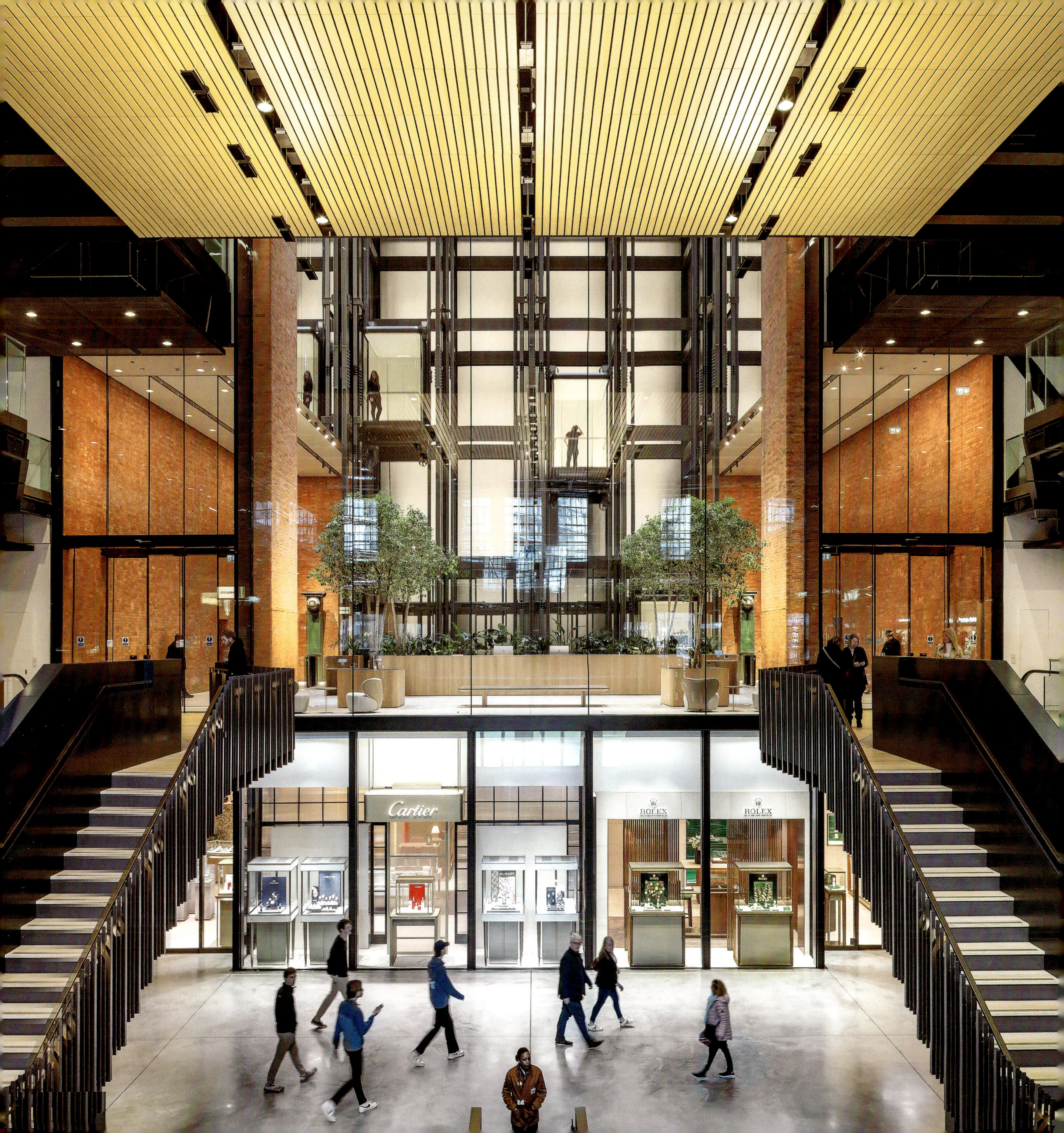

Cartier
ROLEX
ROLEX

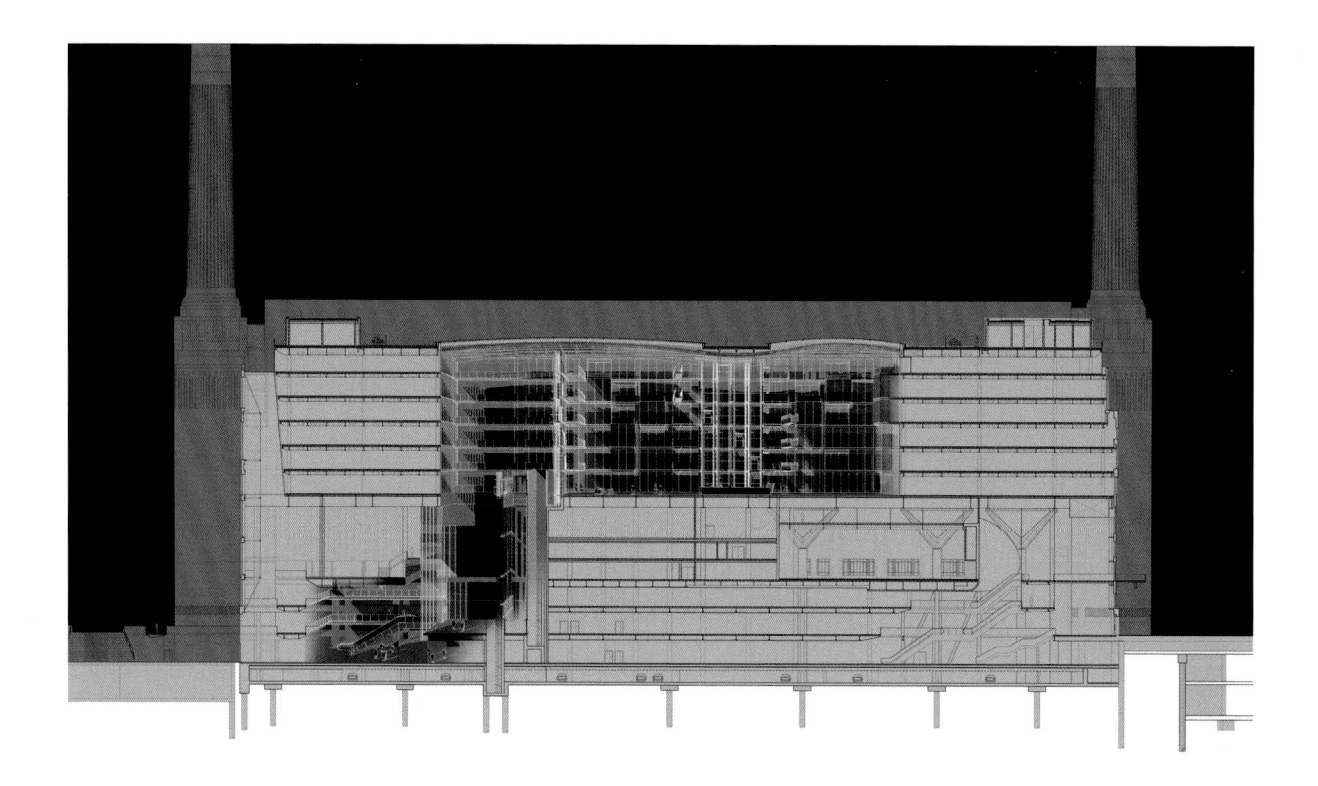

The office component was originally designed to be let to multiple tenants. As such, the atrium space was enclosed, with distinct tenants intended to take up different floors. When Apple came on board as a single occupier, they asked for the office spaces to open out into the atrium. Since the core designs were already in place, this created challenges in terms of evacuation and ventilation. Working with Foster + Partners, the single volume was achieved, including natural ventilation.

The offices benefit from a roof garden on top of Turbine Hall B, which is separated from the private residential gardens with planting and concealed screening.

Writing in 2024, Battersea Power Station Underground Station – designated Zone 1 – is open and running; Apple is now embedded in the Power Station; and, as more phases of the masterplan complete or come forwards, the area is established as a completely mixed-use quarter of London.

opposite Long section highlighting office entrance, sky lobby and atrium

right View of full height windows

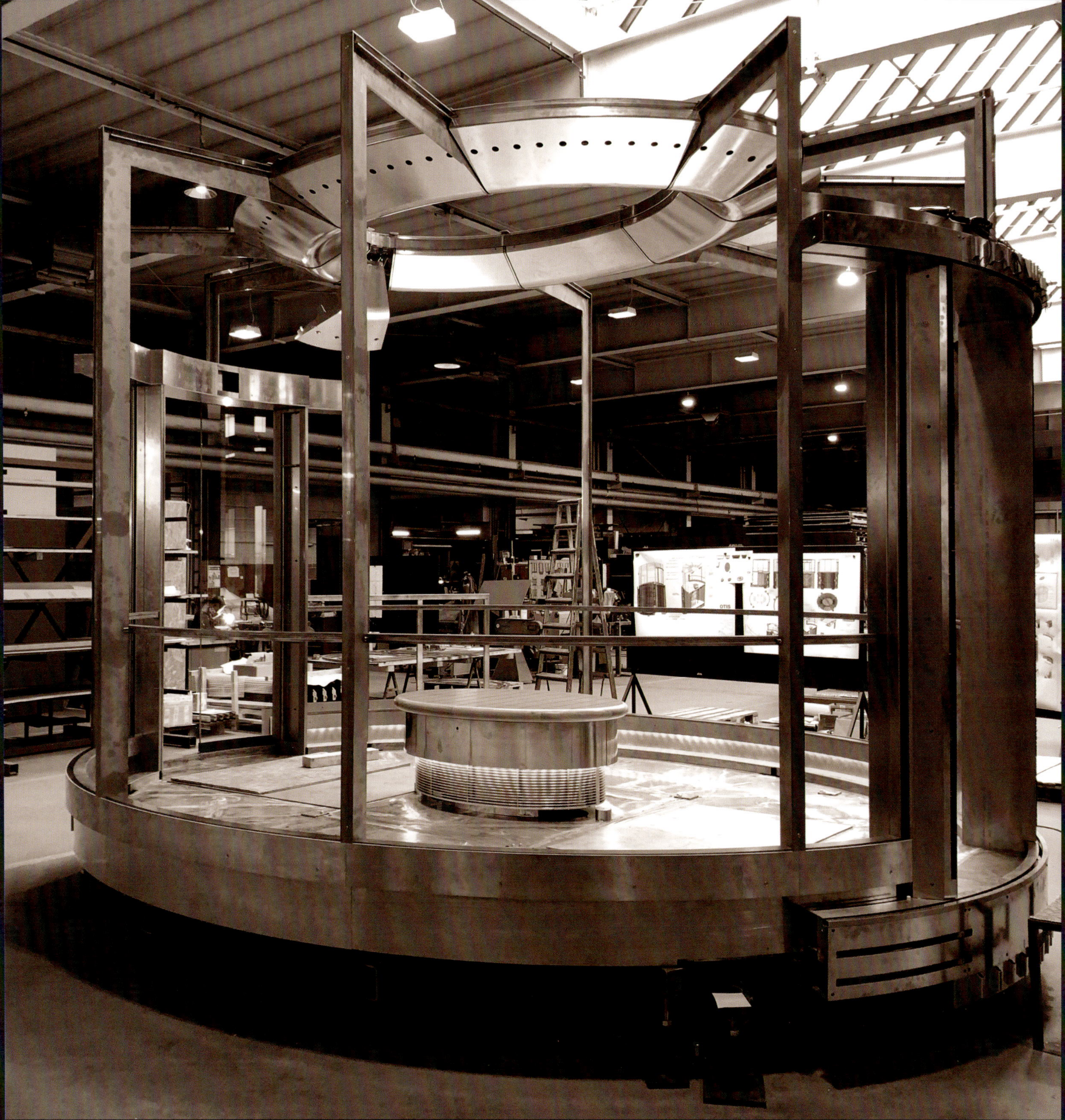
OTIS

Lift 109

Concept Renders

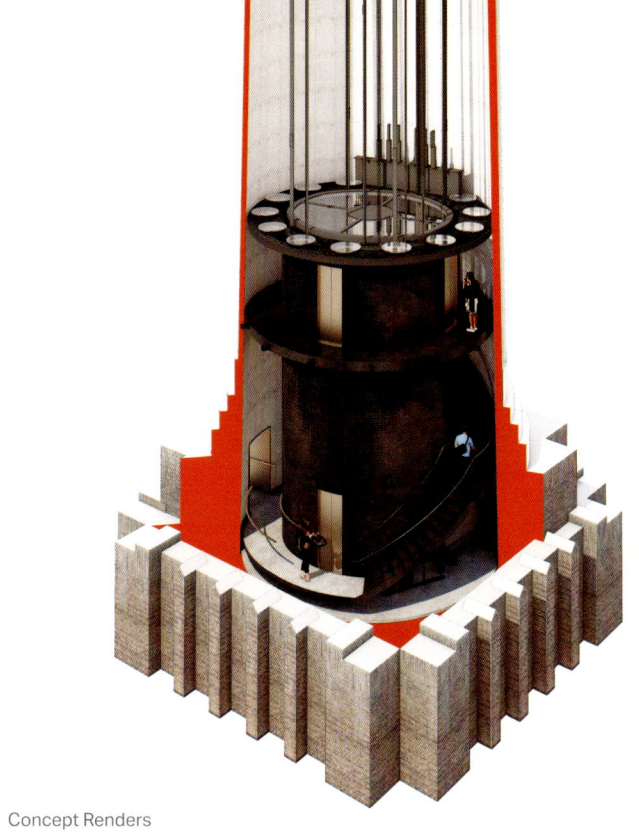

Lift 109 Access Diagram

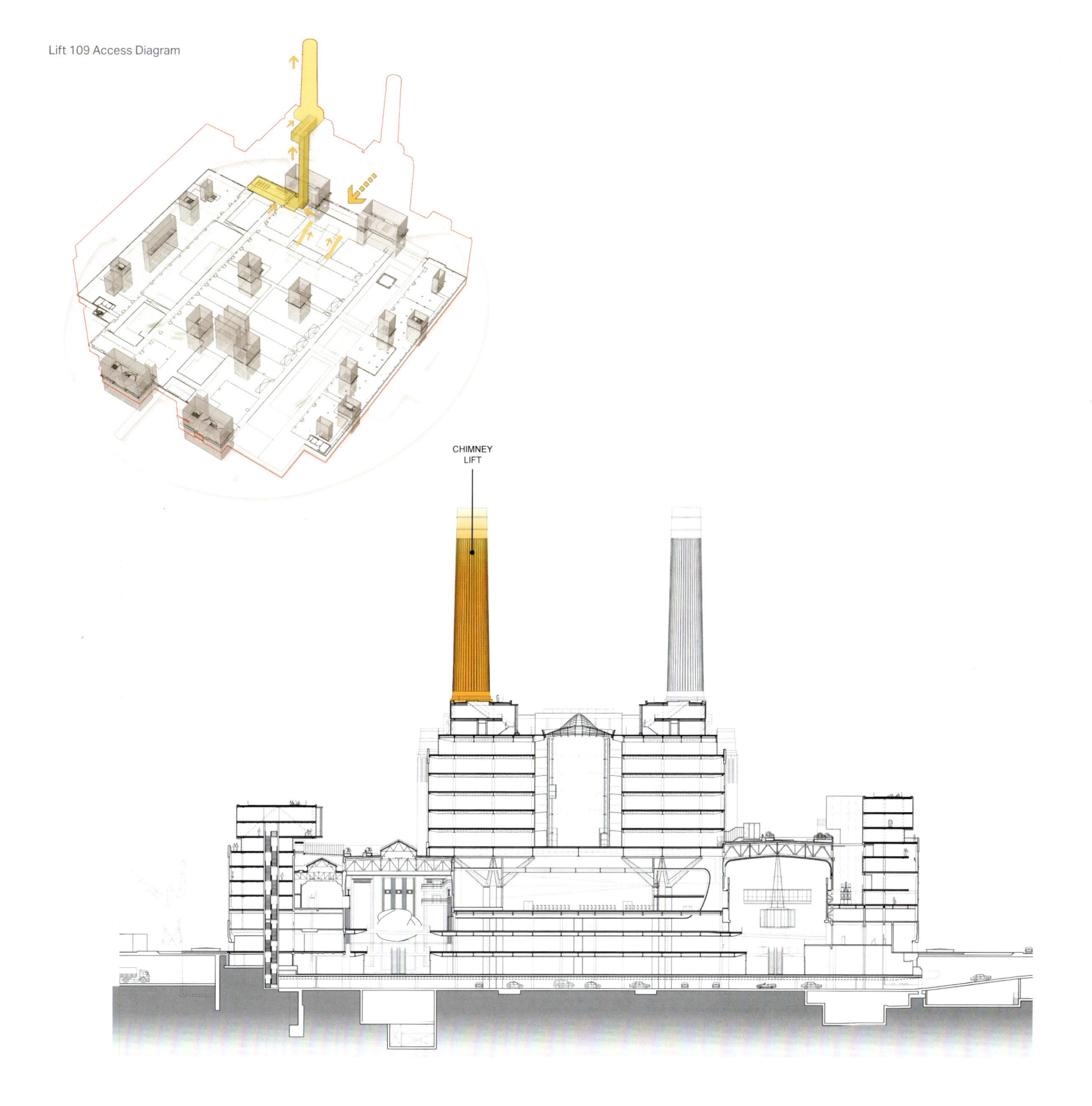

CHIMNEY LIFT

From the inception of the project, there was always an ambition to include a cultural component in the transformation of the Power Station.

In operation, the Power Station had been a dynamic environment containing large-scale plant and many moving components. Although much of this had been lost through decommissioning, the team was keen to ensure that the future life of the building included both a record of the operational processes and carried this dynamic strand through the new experiences.

Elements of this approach can be found throughout the building: in the pieces of equipment that have been restored and displayed as sculpture, including in the public realm; through subtle changes of floor material demarking the former footprint of the turbines; and in the Control Rooms, where the panels form the backdrop to restaurant and event spaces. These components telling the story of operation have been woven into an informal heritage trail that can be picked up by shoppers or followed in full by enthusiasts.

When it came to finding a use for the painstakingly restored but redundant chimneys, a true 'attraction' experience which could potentially generate revenue seemed appropriate. The rebuild of the chimneys had been an enormous undertaking for the client, design and construction team. Expensive and technically challenging, with complicated sequencing, the reconstruction of the four chimneys was paramount to maintaining the iconic silhouette of this London landmark.

Each of the four chimneys is home to a residential lobby, with one chimney also housing 'Lift 109' (named for the 109m height at the top of the lift). The entrance to this lift can be found in Turbine Hall A, where an interactive exhibition gives a brief history of the Power Station. An ordinary lift brings visitors to the base of the chimney where they enter a new highly technical and bespoke glass lift. This lift, in turn, takes visitors up through the chimney itself, emerging out of the top of the chimney and giving 360 views to London.

Putting a lift into a conical chimney presented a number of technical challenges. WilkinsonEyre worked closely with lift manufacturers, Otis, on the bespoke design. With no room for emergency exit stairs in the chimney, one particular challenge was to find a means of evacuation in case of power failure. The solution was found in a second lift, hidden directly below the glass lift, which has the capability of being manually operated in an emergency. To assure their safety, these lifts were tested for 1000s of hours before opening.

To maximise views, the glass lift has a minimal vertical frame. Emerging as it does from the top of the chimney, the lift also had to be designed to withstand an external environment, at height.

Housed directly above one of the lobbies for the Power Station's rooftop residences, Lift 109 is illustrative of the thoroughly mixed-use nature of the building programme and the complexities and challenges that the unusual proximities presented in design. Lift 109 required considerable sound proofing.

Offering an unusual view, from one of the highest viewing points in south-west London, Lift 109 is an extremely popular visitor attraction. Two years on from its opening, it is still regularly fully booked weeks in advance.

117

118

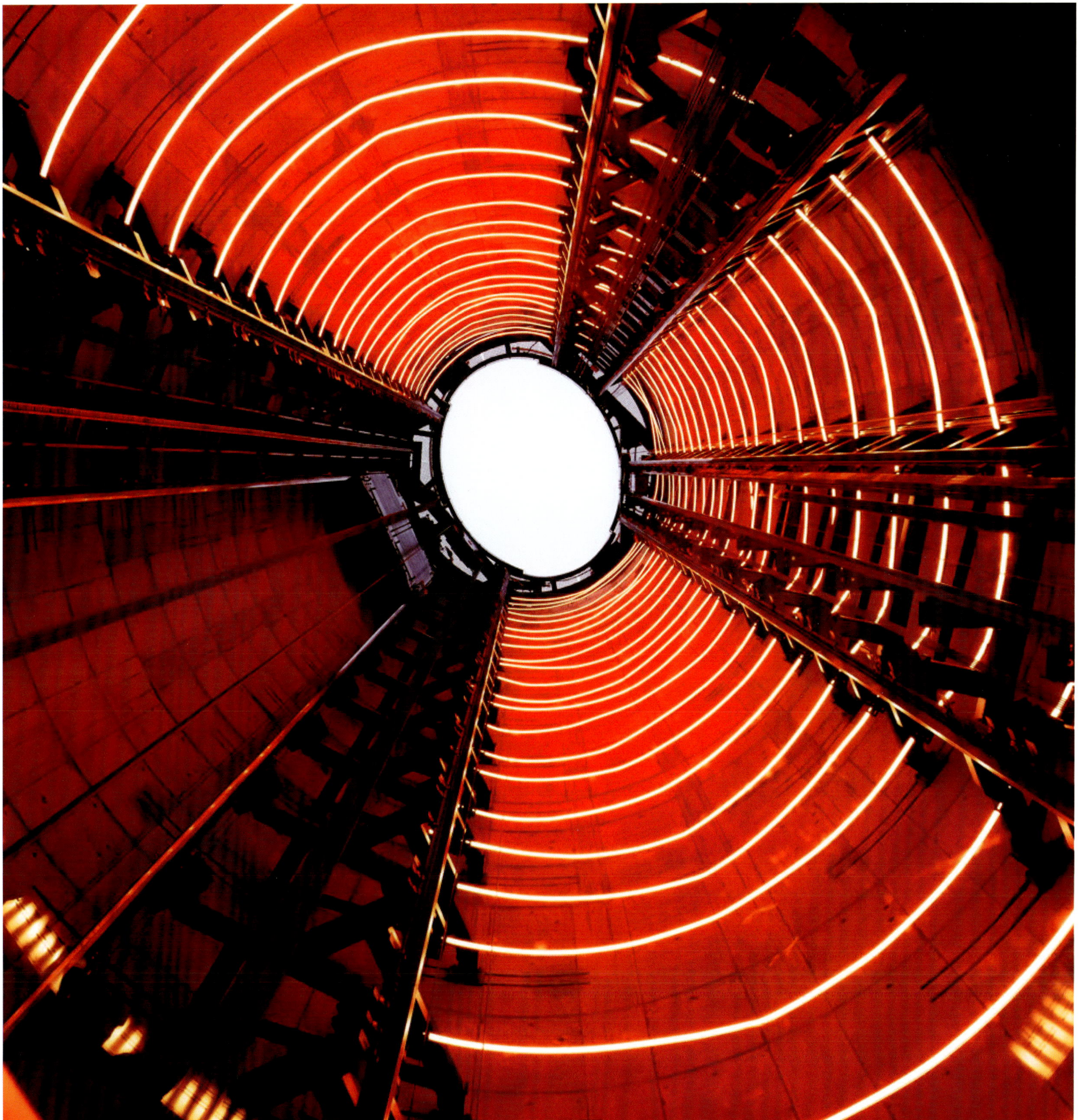

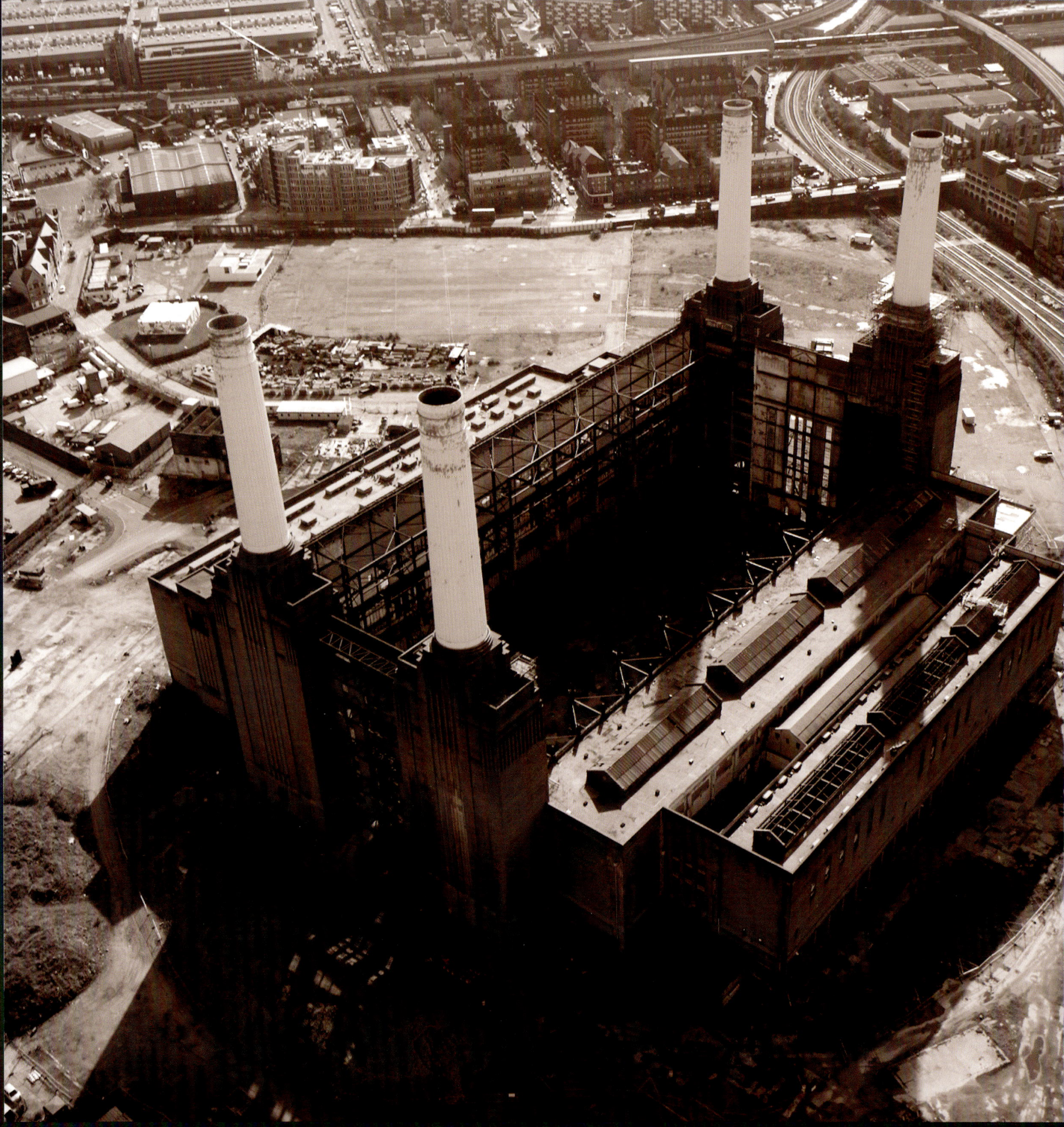

Public Realm

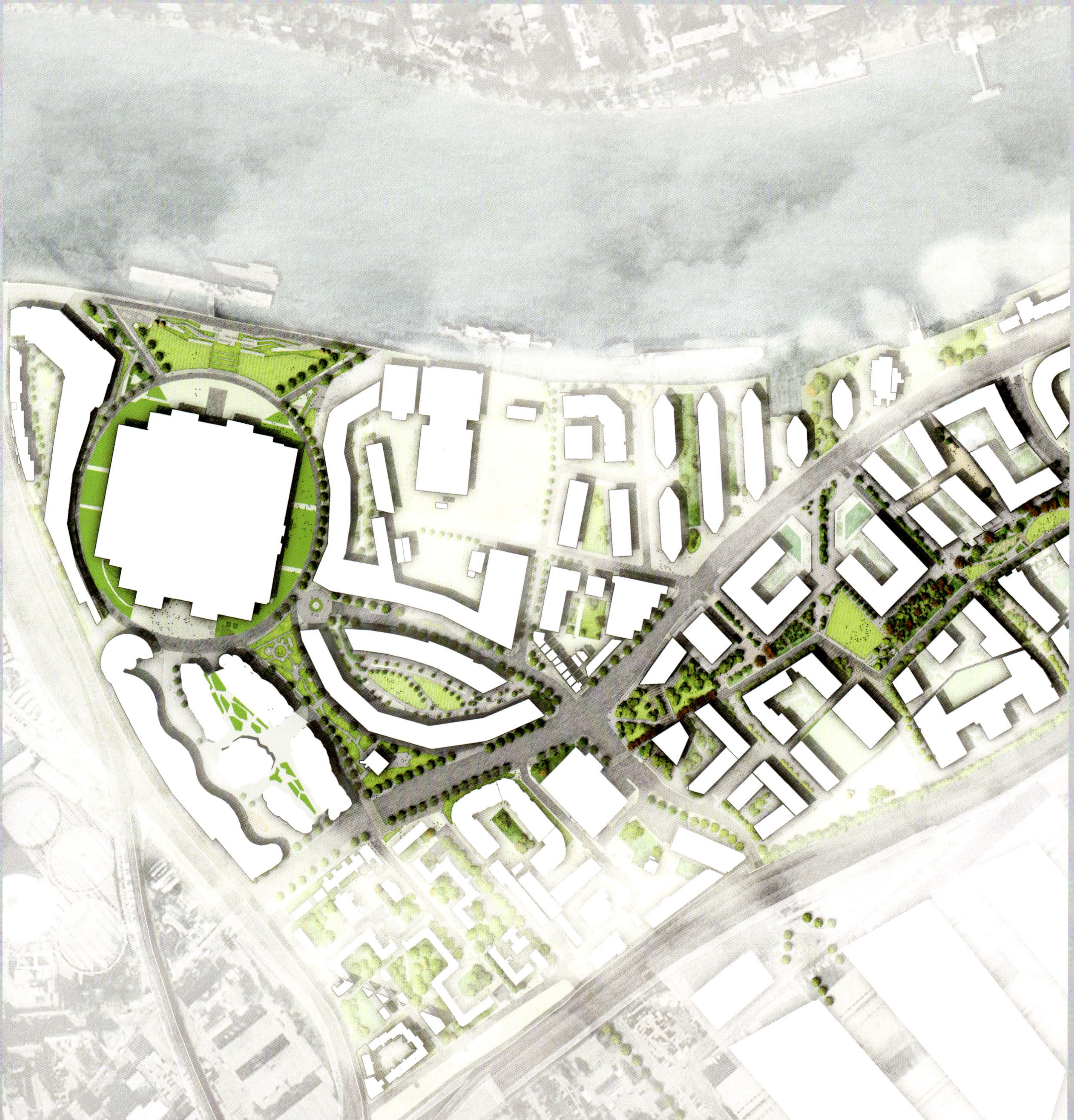

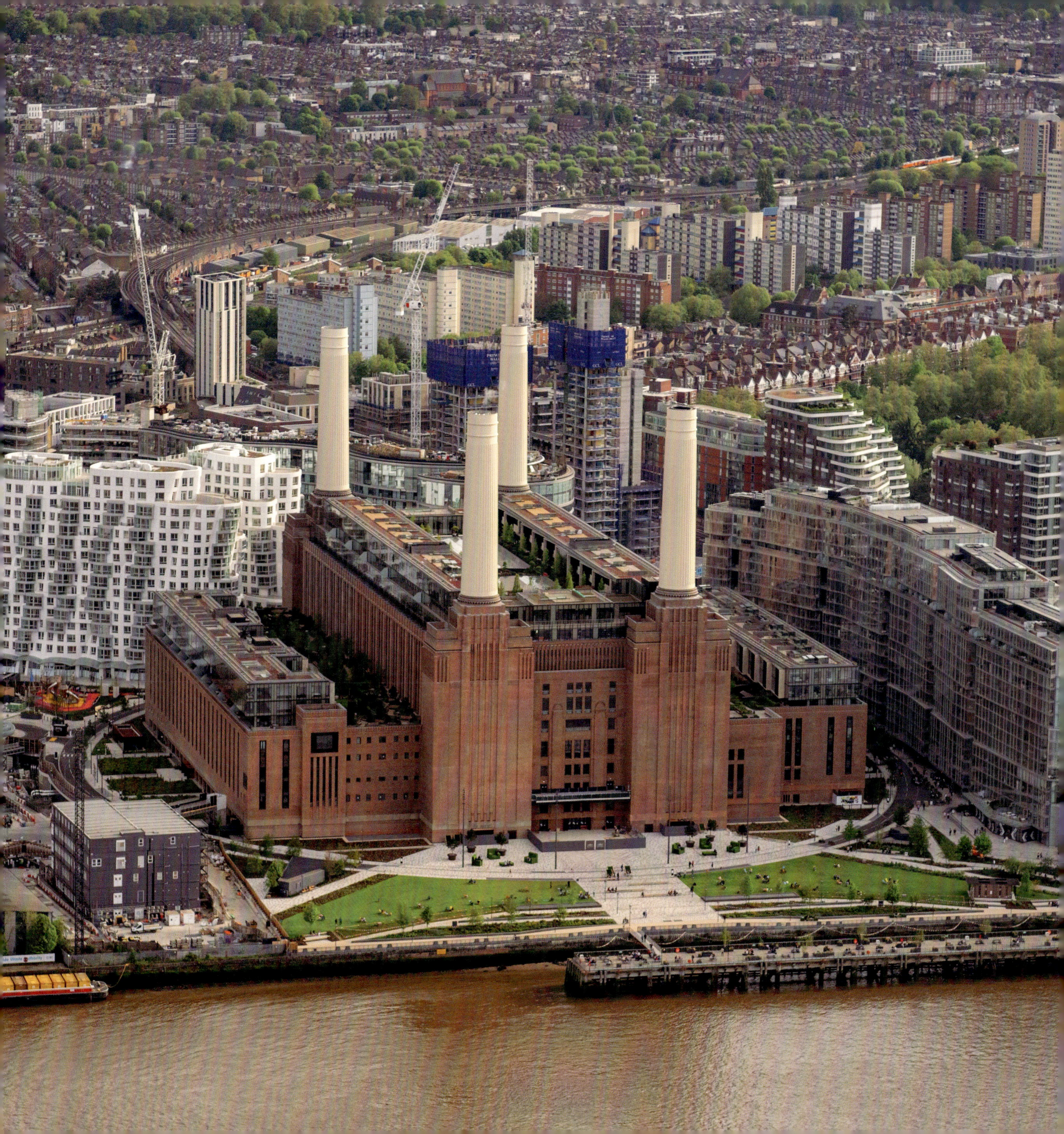

'If a new landscape works, it feels as if it has always been there. Power Station Park feels exactly like this. There's room to soak up the incredible views of the meticulously restored Power Station and space to host large-scale community events.'

Ben Walker, Director,
LDA Design

From the outset of the scheme, Battersea Power Station Development Company understood that, in order to create a viable and vibrant new community in London, the quality of the public realm was of paramount importance.

A 'placemaking' manual was published defining a series of mandates for the project, with 'We don't do ordinary' adopted as the project catchphrase during design and construction. The aim of the manual was to describe a quality standard for the project whilst also carefully establishing the right mix of ingredients and activities to create a buzz and put the Power Station Development on the map.

The Power Station has three key public spaces designed by WilkinsonEyre and LDA:

- The 'Halo Road', a safe haven providing breathing space between the historic fabric and the rest of the development.
- Malaysia Square, an urban public square providing the main entrance to the Power Station arriving from the new tube station and Electric Boulevard.
- North Park, a new public park to the north of the Power Station between the building and the river.

The 'Halo Road's' east and west green spaces create a natural landscaped zone between the building and the access road. LDA developed a strategy of low maintenance and minimal irrigation wild planting, referencing the historic building and its industrial heritage. WilkinsonEyre designed two retail pavilions within these zones. Constructed in mass timber with weathering steel cladding, the units' dedicated terraces spill out into the newly created gardens, bringing human scale to these spaces.

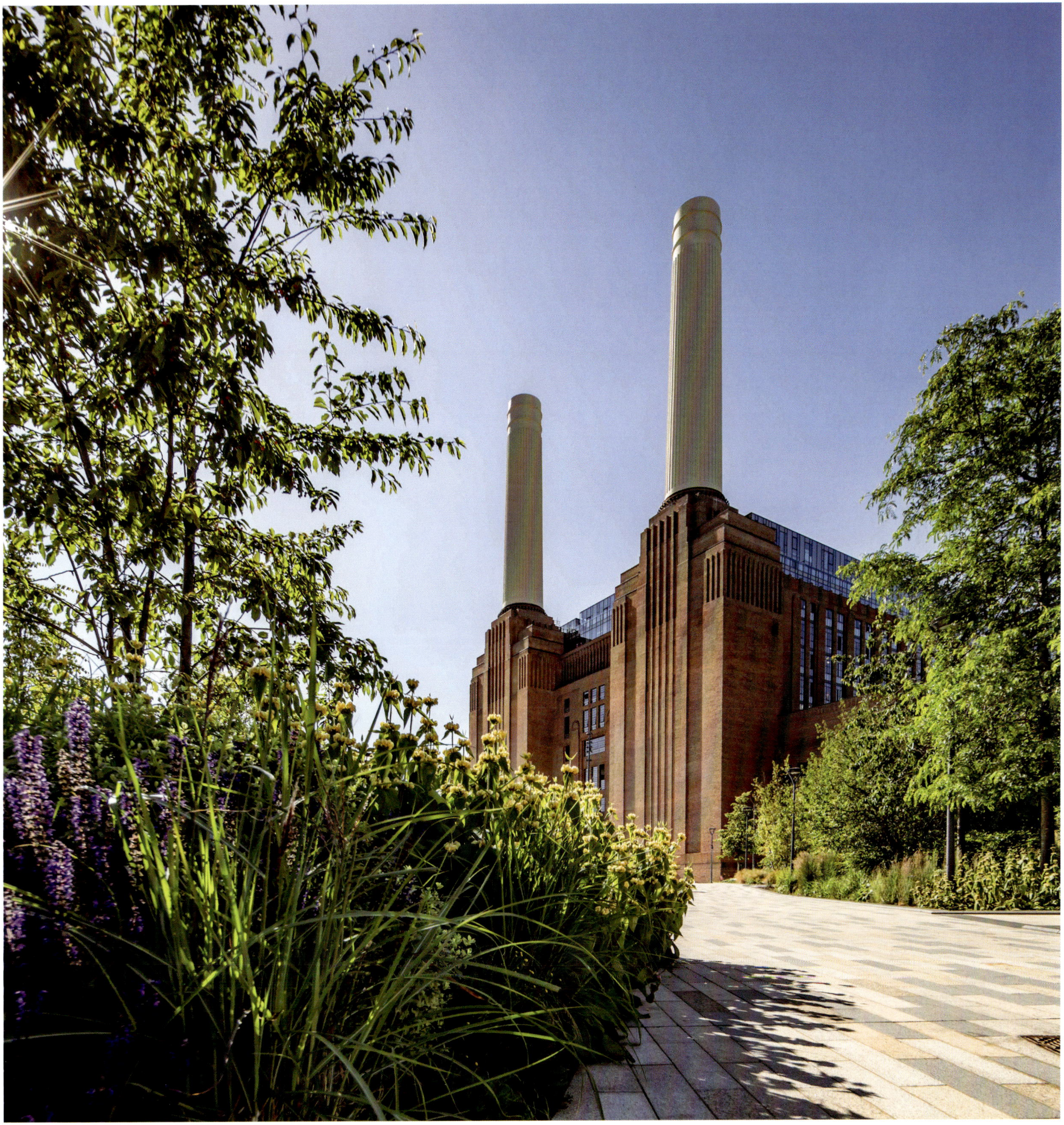

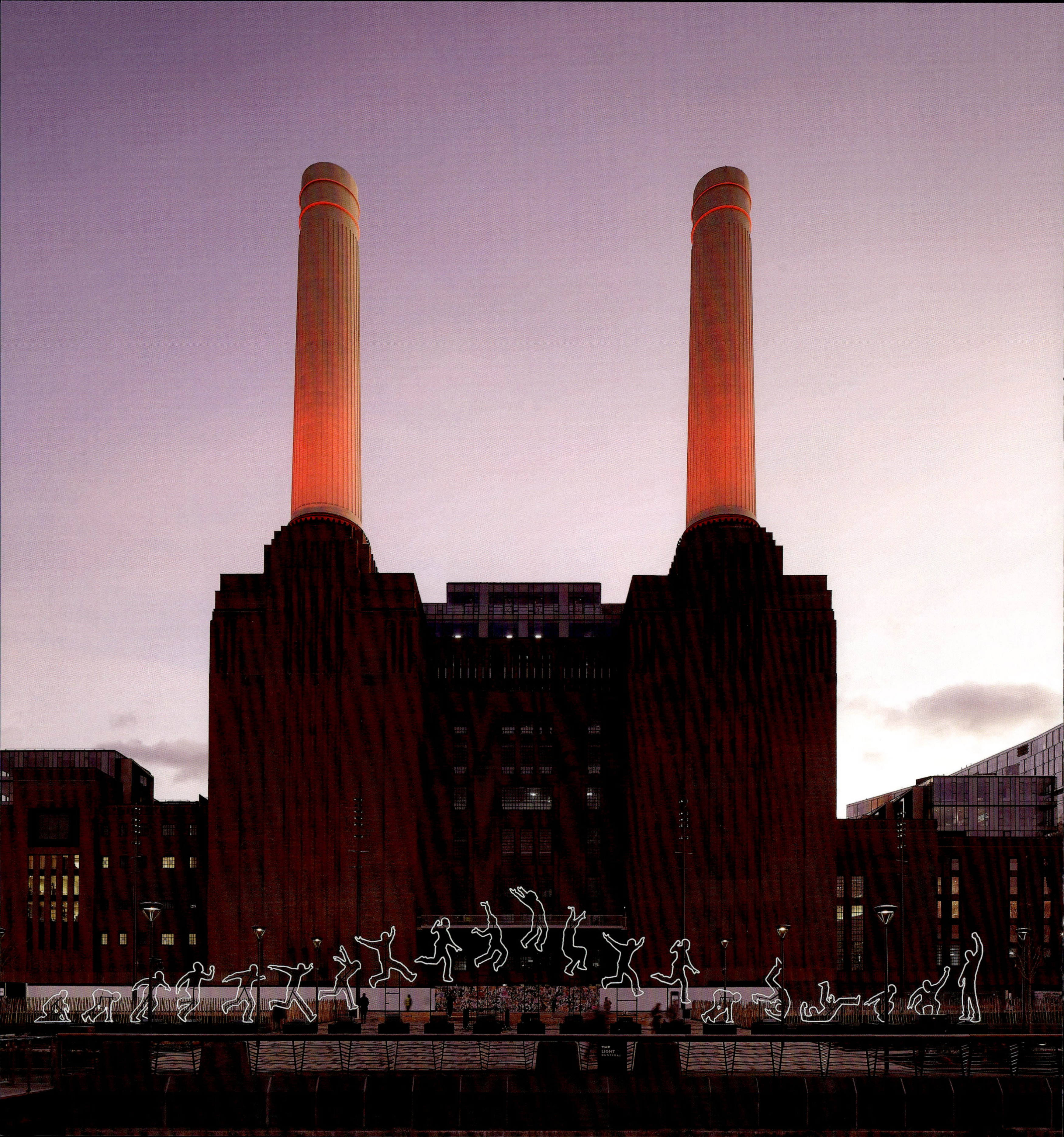

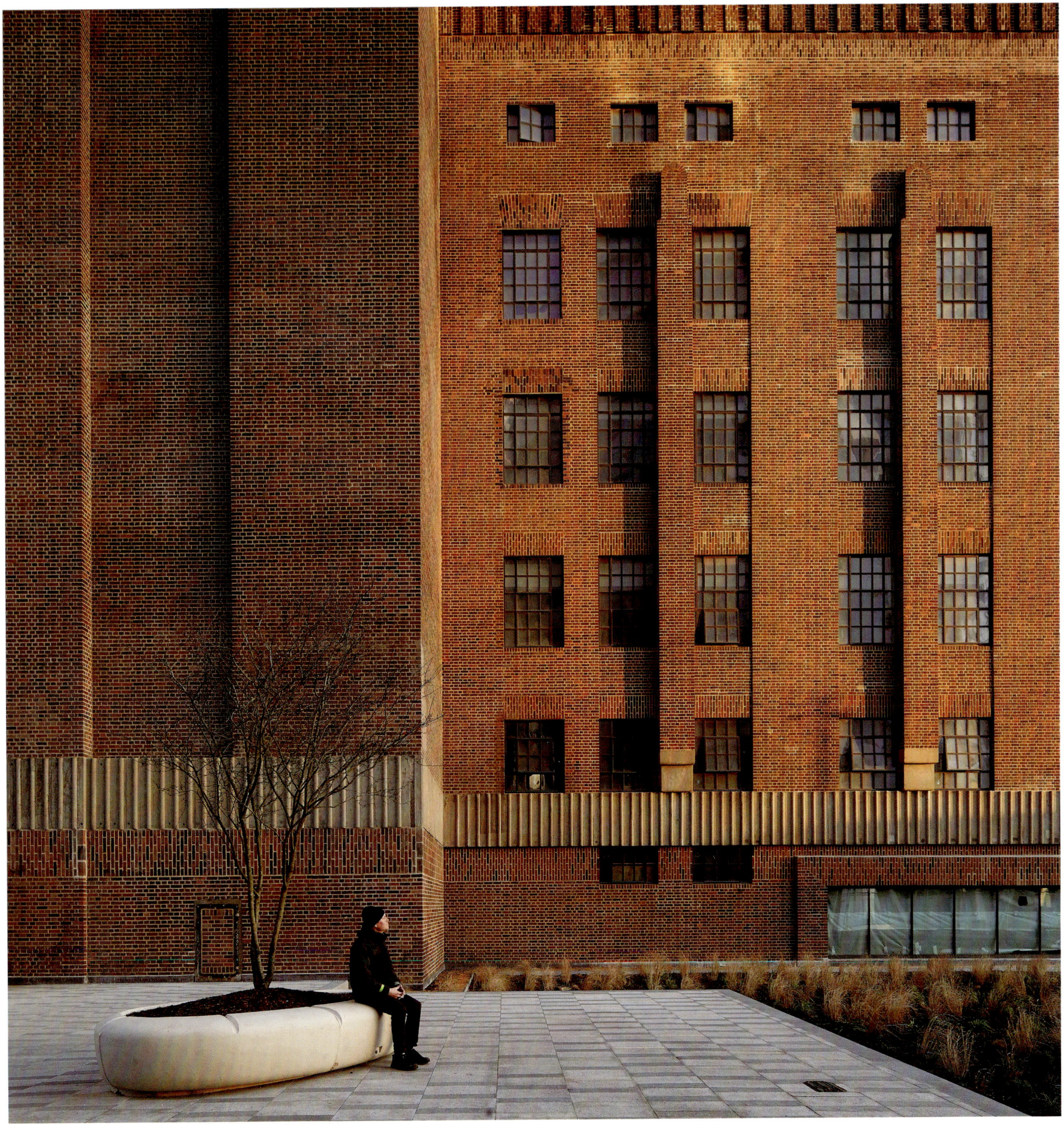

To protect the Power Station and its users from a potential '100-year flooding event,' North Park and the ground level of the building had to be raised one level - approximately 4m in height - from its original entrance level.

At the south entrance of the building, however, where the building connects into Nine Elms and the new tube station, the original ground floor level has been retained. Referencing a the Spanish Steps in Rome, Malaysia Square sits over two levels, resolving the level change and challenge of having two levels of entrance on this side.

Its oval shape accentuates the formality and the symmetry of the Power Station: curved lateral steps carved in granite gently disappear into the lateral walls. A light U-shaped bridge above it forms the Upper Ground entrance to the Power Station keeping minimum interface with the listed walls. The base of the piazza is animated by a programme of external events and activities year-round.

North Park offers a major new park for London alongside the river. Parts of the park are paved, including the zone between the building and the 'Halo Road,' as well as a path from the Power Station to the jetty, in order to facilitate a year-round programme of public events and cultural programming curated by BPSDC. These include outdoor markets, sports events and cultural festivals.

In contrast to Malaysia Square, however, the majority of North Park is covered by lawn, inviting Londoners to lunch or gather there or enjoy the (occasional) bursts of sunshine. The Jetty plays a significant role in the park. In addition to it's use to welcome River Bus users to a new TfL stop, it is used as a gathering spot for specific events, such as the open-air cinema, or as the perfect platform to host temporary kiosks for food and drink or Christmas fairs.

129

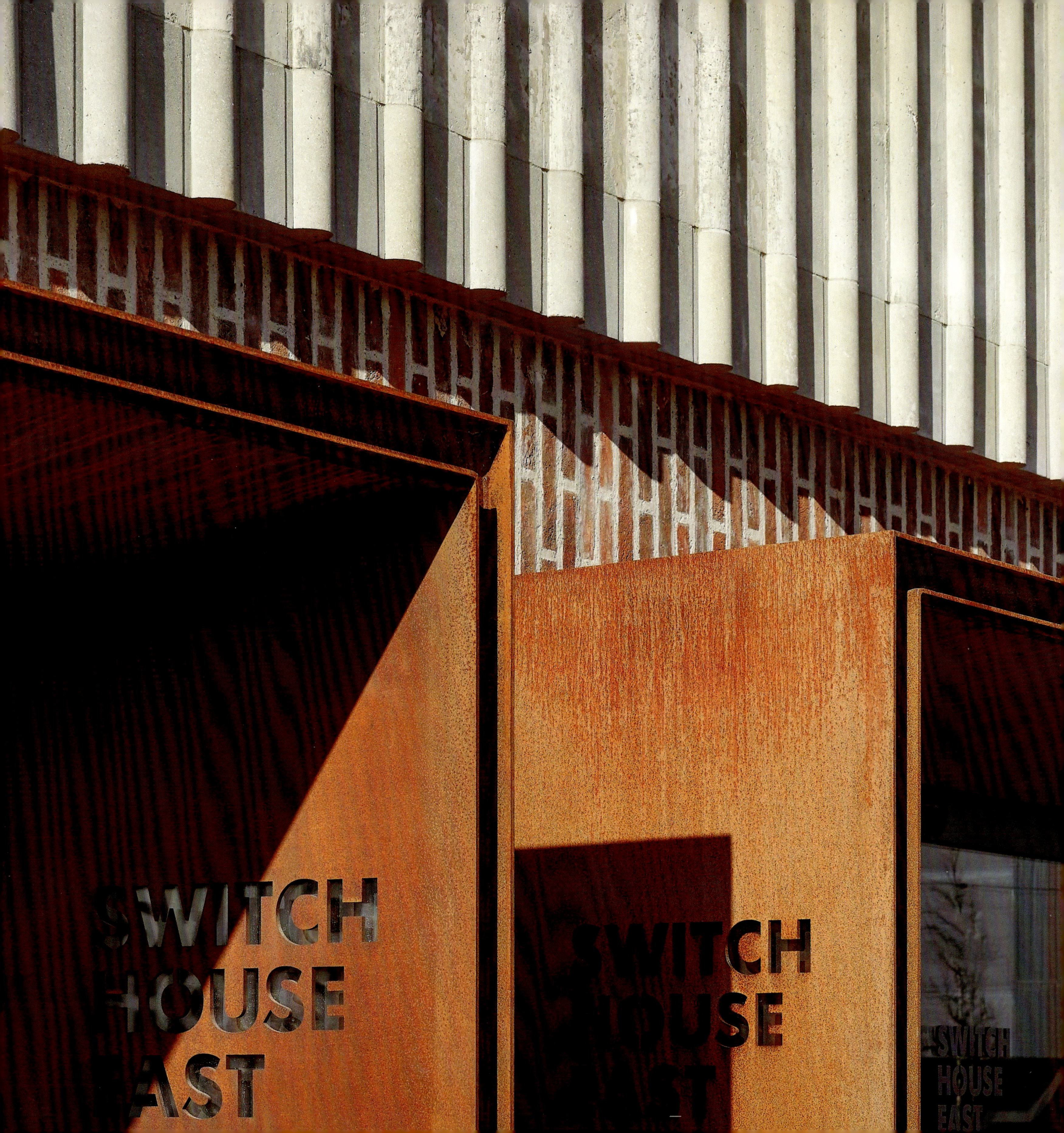
SWITCH
HOUSE
EAST
SWITCH
HOUSE
EAST

Unlocking Challenges

Conservation Stories

left Mortar matching using original suppliers

right Identifying the colour blend to match the original wall

opposite Handmade bricks from the original suppliers

Brickwork Matching

Considered to be one of the largest brick buildings in Europe, the original Power Station was built with over six million bricks from at least six different manufacturers. In order to protect and celebrate the integrity of the existing building, our strategy for brick was to source the original material where possible. Conservation Advisers Purcell worked alongside WilkinsonEyre, with Paye Stonework and Restoration, to repair the original elevations. This enormous task required 1.75 million custom-blended bespoke bricks, including 23 individual brick types in unique sizes.

The Power Station's construction over three phases meant that the brickwork varied substantially and had weathered differently, resulting in a wide variety of tones that needed matching. As luck would have it, the original construction of the Power Station was widely publicised, so WilkinsonEyre were able to trace the original suppliers from contemporary journals, where they had been keen to be associated with the project.

The historic manufacturer for the majority of the exterior bricks was Northwick Brick and Tile, now known as Northcot Brick. Northcot was still working Jurassic Lias from the same quarry that had supplied the Power Station and was even using the same 1920s clay preparation machinery.

The epic restoration and repair process began by mapping the old brickwork to identify the different surface qualities and colours needed for the repairs. Each brick type was assigned a reference number, and drawings were produced to establish the exact percentage required of each.

Through traditional hand throwing, kiln-firing skills, and sophisticated weathering techniques; bricks were manufactured to the correct size, colour, density, strength and porosity and hand-blended in precise ratios to duplicate the original colour palettes.

A team of five master brickmakers made 1.3 million bricks entirely by hand, in two blends, each comprising six or seven brick types to match the exterior pre-war walls.

Internally, other brick types were also sourced from original manufacturers for repairs, including the distinctive buff bricks in Turbine Hall A from Ruabon in North Wales and the 'Nori' bricks, that lined the wash towers, from Accrington. These hard acid resisting bricks were also used for the foundations of the Empire State Building during the same period.

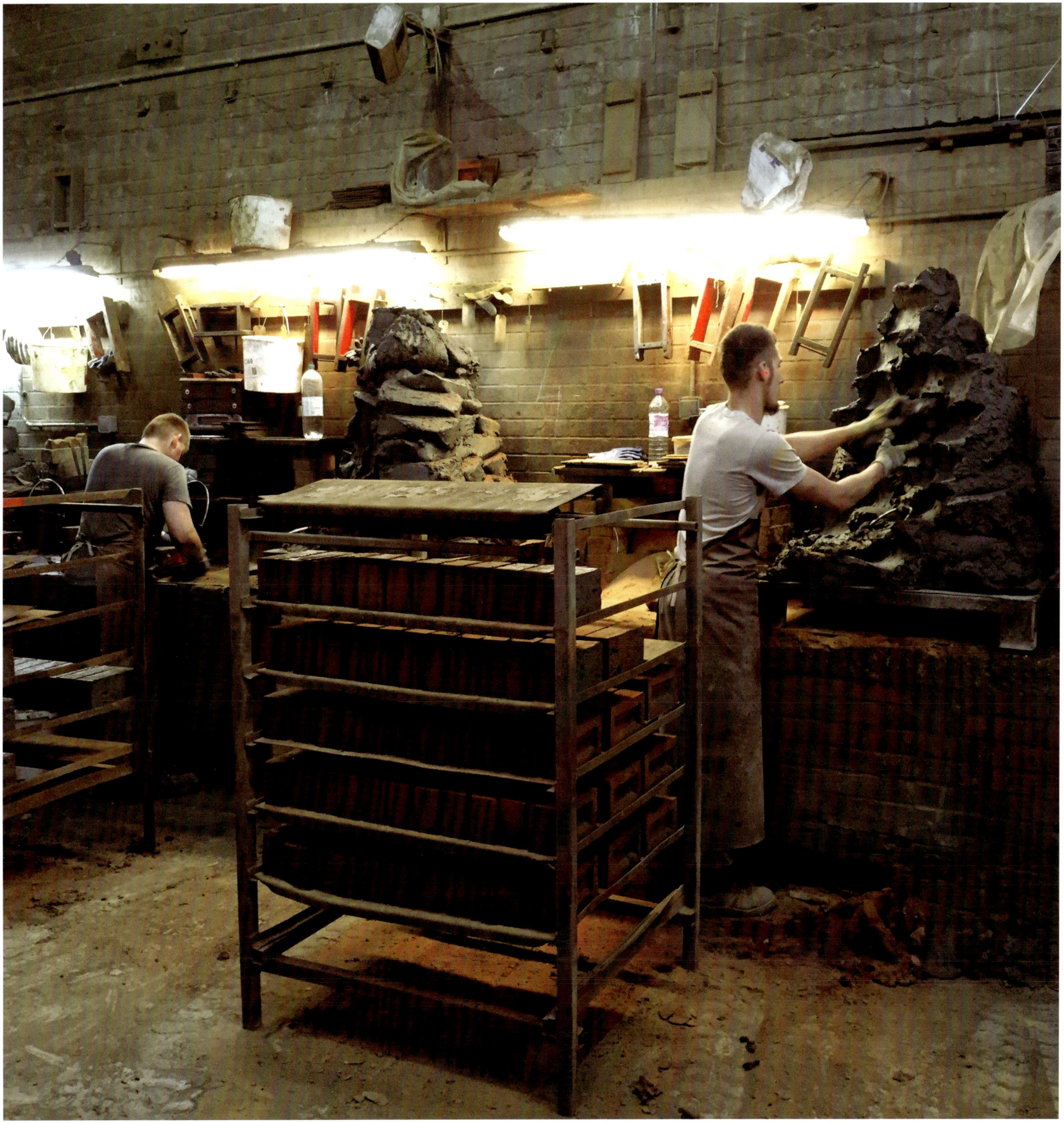

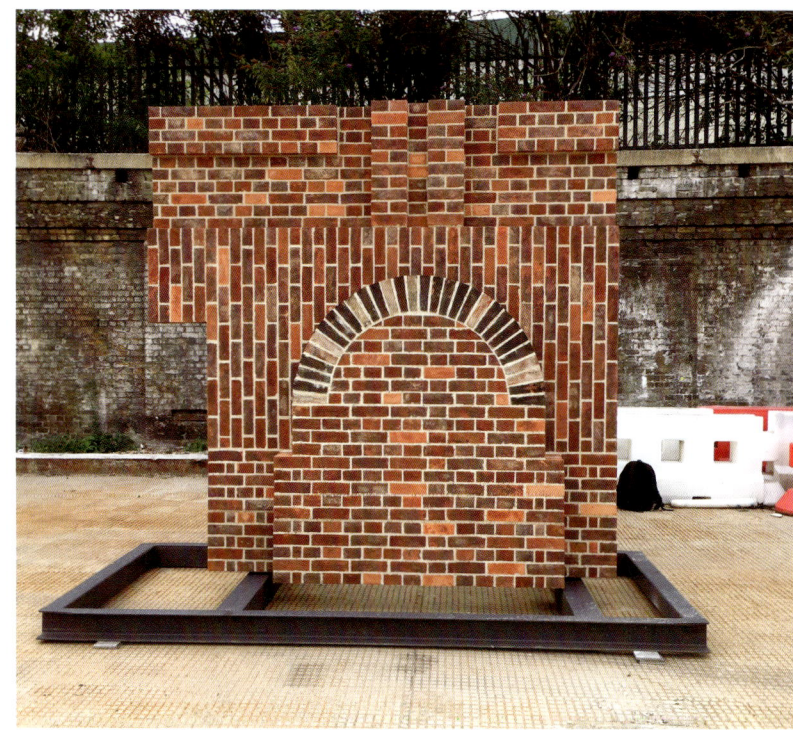

Prefabricated Brickwork

The high-level west wall of the Boiler House had become unstable and been taken down in the 1980s. The remaining east wall was also in very poor condition and consent was obtained to dismantle the wall while recording the detail and salvaging feature bricks to enable a 'like for like' rebuild. As a traditional hand-set wall, five storeys high and starting 25m above ground, this was a very challenging piece of construction with serious logistical and Health and Safety considerations.

WilkinsonEyre set out to research alternative off-site manufacturing techniques and to develop a methodology that could address these challenges and achieve the high quality of brickwork match that was required. WilkinsonEyre developed an innovative prefabricated precast concrete panel system. Constructed off-site by Thorp Precast, it used a mixture of existing and 200,000 matching replacement bricks.

The panels are made using the same bricks and mortar as the original wall. The bricks were cut in half lengthways before being handset into the formwork to match the bonding, before being cast into concrete panels. In this way we could ensure a scholarly recreation of the original within factory conditions. Panels were carefully detailed to minimise and conceal joints. With the reduced thickness of Ultra High-Performance Concrete (UHPC) there was room to introduce more insulation to improve the long term thermal performance of the walls.

This process had to be carried out in very close consultation with the London Borough of Wandsworth and Historic England. It was the first use of a brick faced precast façade system to rebuild an original feature of a Grade II* Listed Building. This is also the first known use of UHPC for a listed façade.

above Prefrabricated sample panels

opposite Prefabricated panels being lifted into place during construction

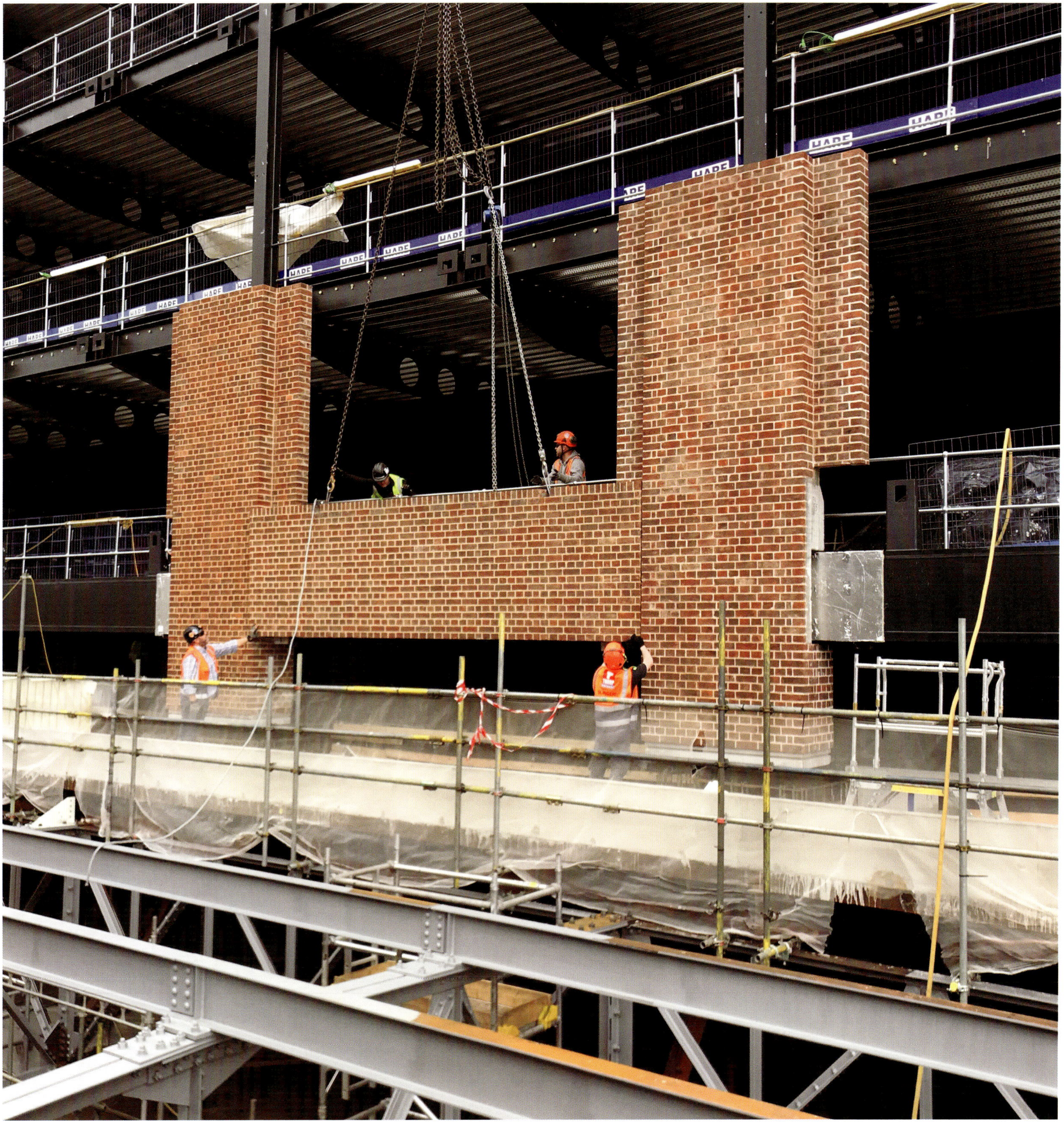

136

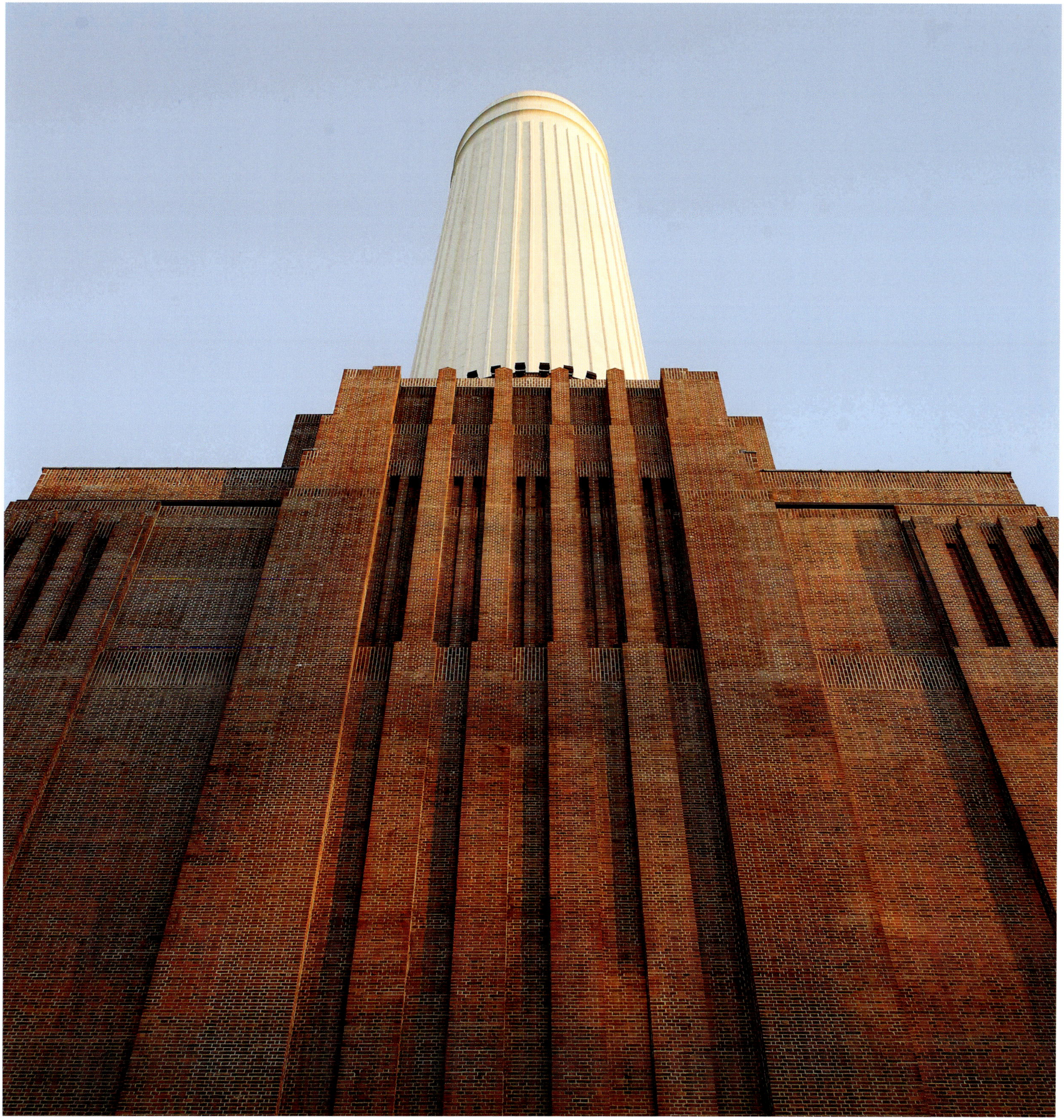

Control Room A

When built, The London Power Company had intended for Control Room A and its grand entrance be a showcase for the Power Station. As such, they were designed with high quality finishes including book-matched marble cladding and parquet flooring, as well as Art Deco flourishes such as the metal and glass ceiling and bespoke light fittings. Contemporary observers commented that is was more like the dining room of an ocean liner than the control room of a power station.

This original dual-purpose - part working environment part visitor attraction - inspired our approach to conservation which sought to strike a balance between the restoration of the highly decorative finishes whilst retaining the wear of experience found in the functional elements such as the control panels with their levers and dials. To enable the room's new use as a unique event space where visitors can engage with the enigmatic control panels, each had to be individually assessed to understand what safety and conservation measures were necessary without risking over-repair that could harm any character.

The success of the new use also required the integration of modern services in as light and inobtrusive a way as possible. This was achieved by understanding and taking advantage of some of the original strategies employed when they were first installed, such as running heating pipework in the ceiling and reusing decorative grilles as diffusers. All services were meticulously planned within the repaired art deco ceiling.

Materials for repair were carefully sourced throughout to match the original including, for example, five types of stone, one of which was recovered from historic stock from an exhausted quarry. Some original methods were used alongside innovative techniques, such as laser printing to match highly specific handles to control panels.

above From top left, marble replacement, restored chevron pattern parquet, restored control panel and glass ceiling

opposite Control Room A fully restored

139

Control Room B

Control Room B contains the reporting and recording equipment that was necessary to monitor the output of Turbine Hall B. Built a decade after Control Room A, during wartime, it continues the faience tiling of the turbine halls but to a simpler more utilitarian design adopting an austere wipe-clean aesthetic with curved corners and steel finishes.

The space is dominated by a distinct arc of stainless-steel control panels that remain substantively intact from when they operated. All methods and materials for cleaning and repair had to be trialled and then reviewed with London Borough of Wandsworth and Historic England before being carried out. Many of these were unique tasks such as the conservation cleaning of dials or the replacement of removable fuses (containing asbestos) with a visually matching but safe plastic drum.

Since the room fronts onto Turbine Hall B, almost like a theatrical set, the new design sought to celebrate this connection. For safety and conservation reasons, the panels in Control Room B required a higher level of management of public access compared to Control Room A: minimal curved glass screen provides display to the public whilst offering the appropriate long-term protection for the panels.

above Control panels carefully dismounted and restored

opposite Control Room B fully restored

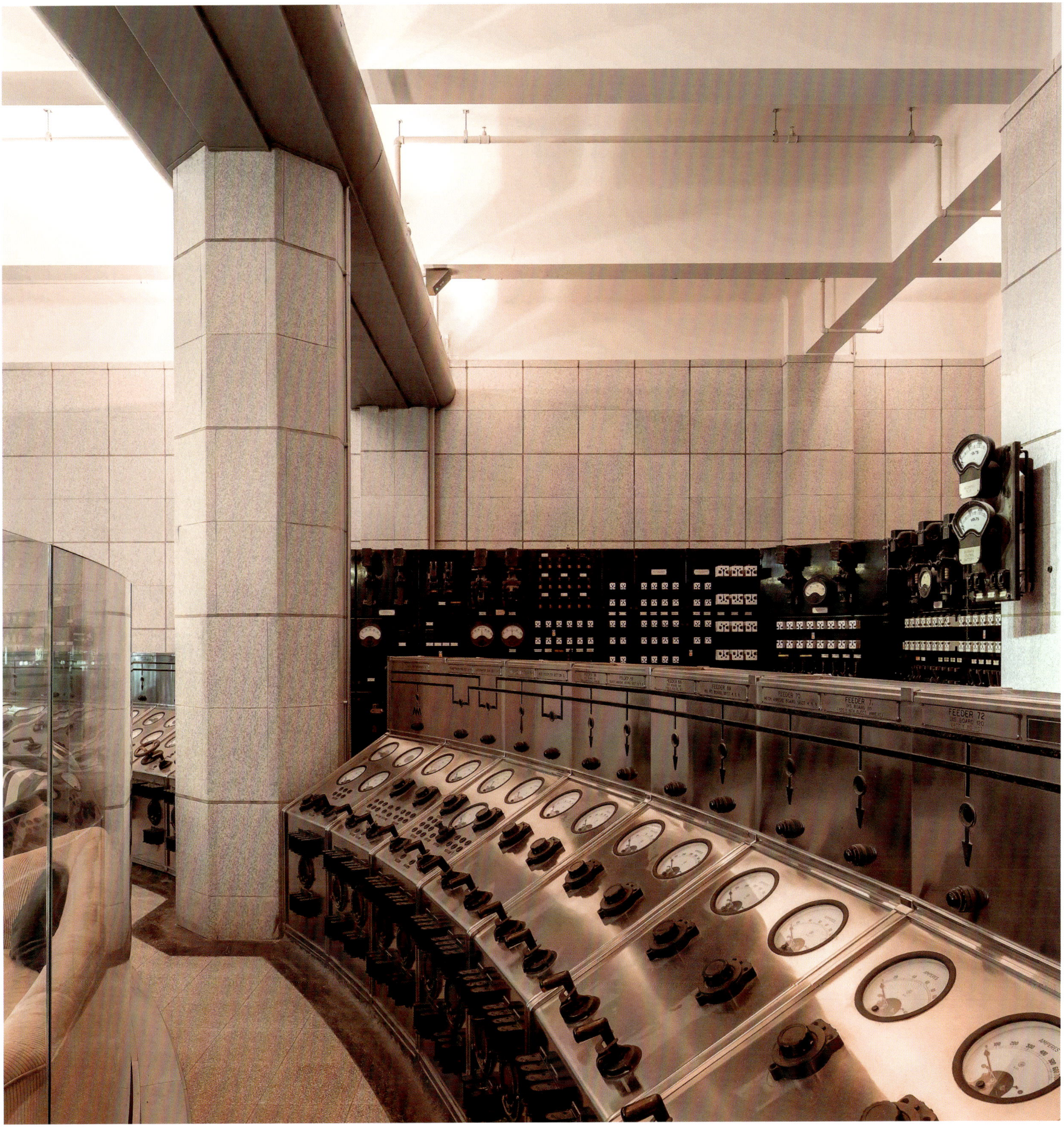
FEEDER 69
FEEDER 70
FEEDER 72
AMPERES

The Chimneys

The four chimneys are the defining feature of Battersea Power Station on the London skyline. As its most iconic elements, ensuring their long-term future was essential to the successful reuse of the Power Station.

Following many years of neglect, close examination showed the reinforced steel within the concrete had corroded and the chimneys were in a very fragile state, covered in small cracks like an old porcelain vase. After trialling different ways of repairing the chimneys over many years, it became clear that the only way to safeguard them for future generations was to dismantle and rebuild them.

The expectation is that, with periodic maintenance, the rebuilt chimneys will last well into the next century before requiring any major repairs.

To meet planning conditions, one of the chimneys had to be rebuilt successfully before work could begin on the other three. Work therefore began with the south-west chimney, and it was only once it had been reconstructed to a height of 25m above the brick wash tower that work was able to begin on the three remaining chimneys.

Each chimney was dismantled using a circular rigging solution, descending the chimney slowly from the top, chipping away at the material and safely removing the debris for partial reuse. Once each chimney had been dismantled it was rebuilt from the bottom, using the same form of reinforced concrete materials as the original, but improving the pattern of the steel reinforcement and the composition of the concrete to make the chimneys less vulnerable to corrosion and to ensure longevity.

The exteriors of the chimneys are visibly identical to the original including the fluting, ornate detail and even the concrete joint lines. The original paint was sampled and analysed so that an accurate match could be found.

WilkinsonEyre set out to ensure the chimneys remained a functional part of the whole design and so each one has a variety of new uses that have required new elements on the inside of the chimneys. All four form part of the access lobbies to the residential apartments on the roof of the Boiler House, with three of them allowing a view directly up the chimney through a central glazed oculus. Two are still used for the discharge of flue gases from the new Power Station Energy Centres with maintenance access to the top. The north-west chimney now contains Lift 109 - a unique visitor attraction that provides the public with the possibility of emerging from the chimney for the view.

opposite View of the chimney highlighting jump formed construction

right Chimneys rebuilt one by one

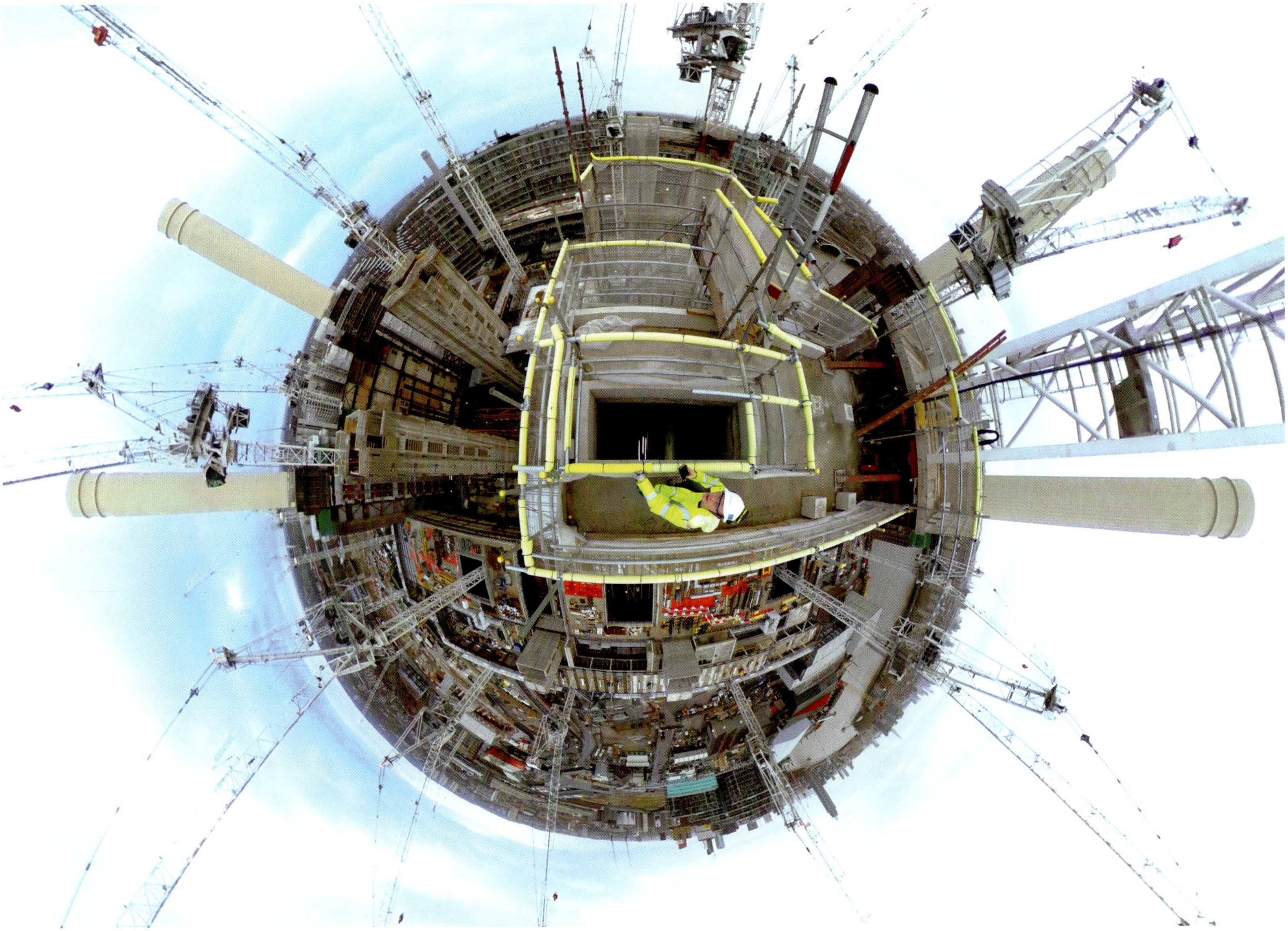

opposite View from the Power Station summit

right Chimneys fully restored

Gardens in the Sky

The scale of Battersea Power Station, with a footprint of approximately 150m x 150m, coupled with the collapsed Boiler House roof, offered the perfect opportunity to rethink the roof design and to introduce something that engaged with the new activities being created in the building.

The three main roofs are above the Boiler House, Turbine Hall A and Turbine Hall B. Directly accessible from the adjacent new residential properties, they have been transformed into new communal gardens for residents and office workers.

Each roof posed individual problems but, in order to enable the creation of a roof garden, the universal challenge was putting enough soil on the top of a listed structure whilst retaining as much of the existing listed fabric as possible. In order to plant mature trees, an average of depth of 500mm of soil was required.

Turbine Hall A is the most sensitive roof structure, with light metal trusses spanning across the faience clad walls. Adding a roof garden and reglazing the rooflight with well insulated double-glazed units meant adding significant weight to the original structure. Working closely with Buro Happold Structural Engineers, the design team managed to justify reinforcing the metal trusses by adding metal plates to some of their bottom flanges.

The original concrete roof, vastly damaged by years of neglect, was replaced by a new metal deck with concrete infill, which allowed the additional volume of soil and paving required to create a vibrant new garden. This work was undertaken using a temporary suspended deck supported from the existing gantry beams which span each bay. The deck moved from north to south while the work was completed, allowing restoration work in Turbinal Hall A to take place in parallel.

A different approach was chosen for Turbine Hall B where the existing roof construction was in poor condition with extensive contamination. The existing 3m deep ceiling void offered the opportunity to house major plants for the retail units below, as such making it a major part of the infrastructure for the building. These combined considerations necessitated a fundamental rethink of the roof structure which then allowed the integration of other new components.

Replacement trusses were set out on the original grid to support the weight of the roof gardens. The ceiling was a key feature of Turbine Hall B, so was replaced with a visually identical replica but in modern construction was achieved at less 20 percent of the weight helping to offset the weight increase of the garden. The new roofing allowed for the whole area to be fully insulated and light tubes set out to follow the original vent locations now bring daylight down into the Turbine Hall below.

The roof of the Boiler House is completely new and sits above a new structure supporting 12 storeys of accommodation: a combination of retail, event spaces, six storeys of offices and the lateral residential villas. The constraints on this roof were therefore completely different. Here, WilkinsonEyre needed to bring in as much natural light as possible into the major office component below. An enormous 80x20m flat glazed roof was integrated above the six-storey internal 'street' in the office space. This huge, glazed component sits on a continuous upstand and acts as smoke vent and natural ventilation for the office space. It is one of the most significant and complex glazed roofs constructed in recent years.

The design of the new 'Gardens in the Sky' was essential for the new residents, workers and visitors to the Power Station in wellbeing, sustainability, and biodiversity terms. With the help of Andy Sturgeon Landscape Architects, we have created a new London square on top of a building.

opposite left Boiler House villas under construction

opposite right Historic equipments located in courtyard

right Turbine Hall B roof garden

left Switch House East courtyard

below Detail of Turbine Hall B roof garden with dome of light tube below

opposite View across the city from Turbine Hall B roof

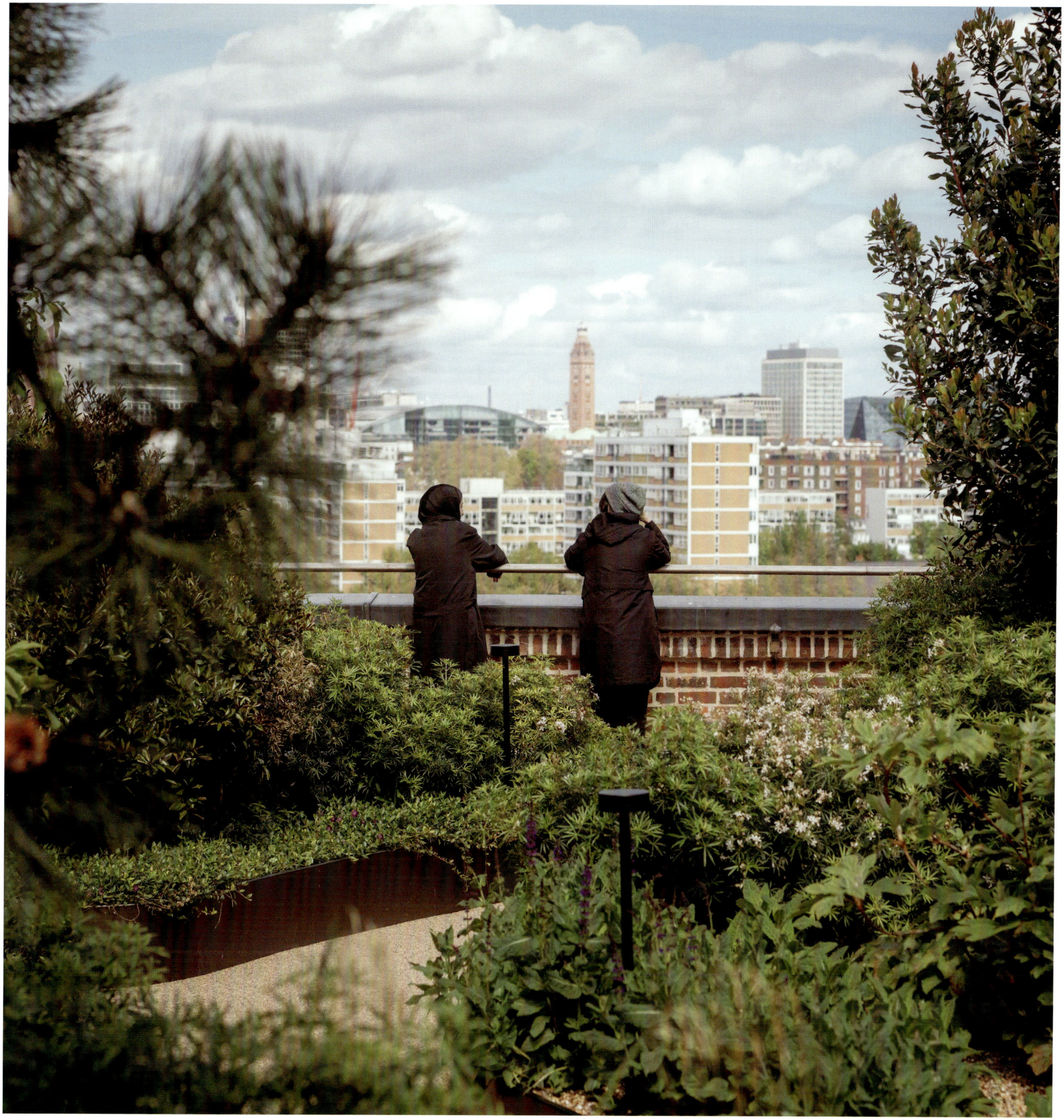

Peregrine Falcon

The Power Station had been home to Peregrine Falcons for more than 20 years and they are a common sight at the top of the north-west chimney looking down across the Thames towards the City.

WilkinsonEyre worked with BPSDC's Peregrine expert, David Morrison of London Peregrines, to design a new permanent home within the Grade II* Listed building for its fastest residents.

Peregrine Falcons occupy a number of the best vantage points on the London skyline. As a protected species, nest boxes are therefore commonly provided to ensure they are not disturbed during nesting, which is a criminal offence. Typically, falcon accommodation takes the simple form of a metal box in a location away from people. At the Power Station, however, bolting a box onto the iconic chimneys or onto the most prominent listed façade was not an option.

Having understood the falcon's territorial habits and how they use clifflike façades with ledges to teach fledglings to fly, a location was identified away from occupied areas where an existing vent opening could be adapted.

Internally this meant a quarrying style operation to form an appropriately sized opening within solid concrete and steel. The falcon's box is accessed through an unidentified door in a WC area with an acoustic lobby to ensure the peregrines are not disturbed by internal activity. The nest contains power and data for a set of cameras which provide a live video feed, along with water and drainage to allow the nest box to be cleaned.

Having moved into temporary accommodation provided by BPSDC during the construction work, the peregrines have now taken up residence in their new permanent home and seem to be delighted with their unique riverside terrace.

opposite above Initial sketch of Peregrine Falcon nest

below Peregine Falcon in its new habitat

151

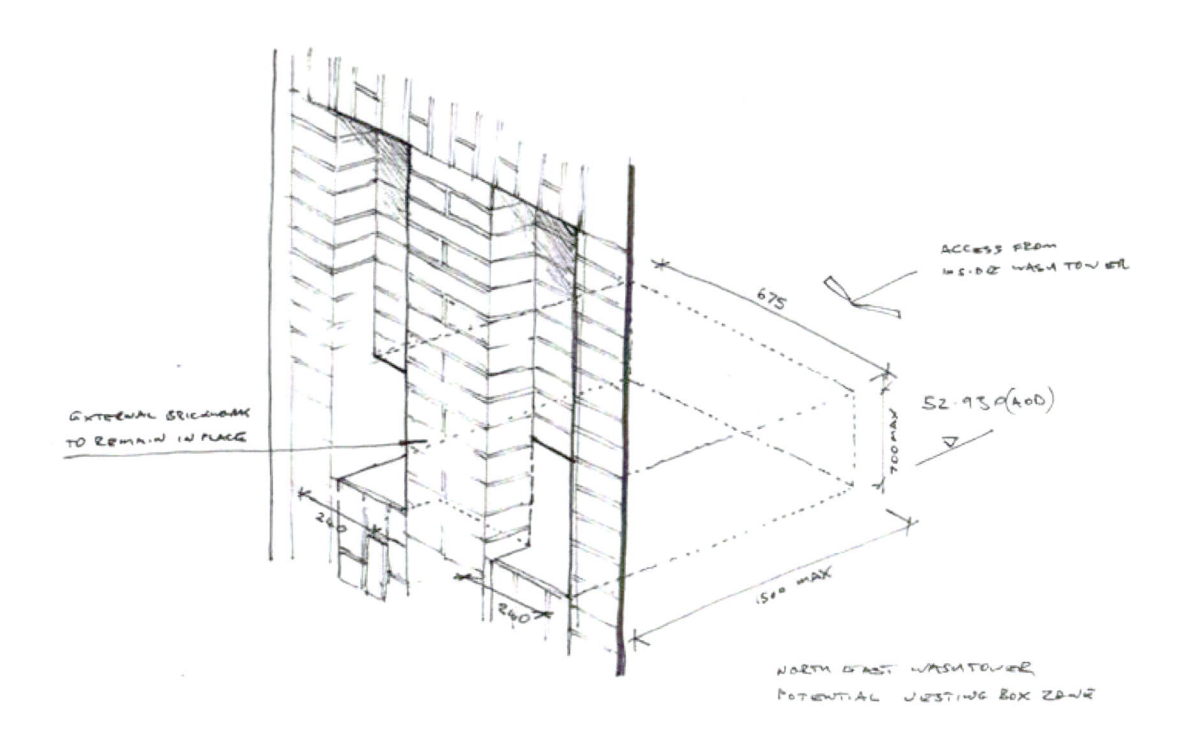

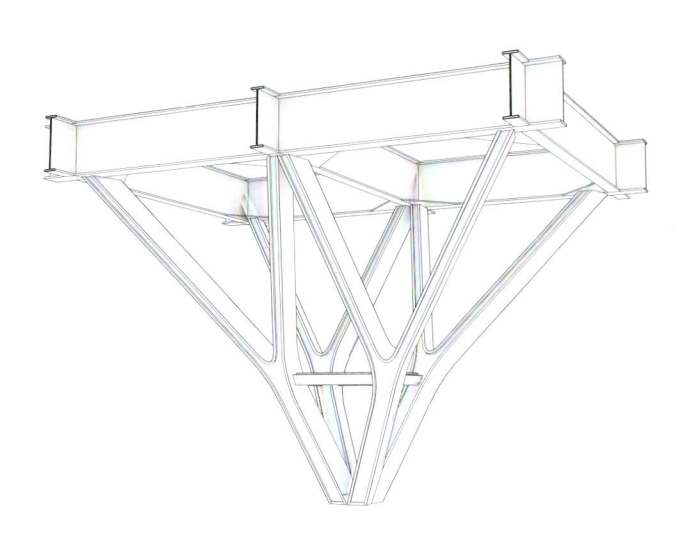

Tree Column Structures

The main event space and associated grand lobby planned at the heart of Battersea Power Station needed to be column-free to maximise flexibility and celebrate the internal fabric of the Power Station's existing north wall. This was made possible by full storey height trusses concealed within plant floors and a pair of 'Tree Columns': Reaching three stories high the column's 'branches' spread out to collectively carry the load of twelve columns from the office space above.

To carry the significant loads, the branches needed to be fabricated from steel plate up to 150mm thick. Challenges came when the curved elements had to be formed in these heavy steel plates. The design had to be tuned to fit the parameters of the fabrication tools available. The transportation of such large elements from Yorkshire to West London had to be carefully considered as part of the tree structure design. Any division of the members required full thickness structural welds on site with invisible joints.

The Tree Columns have two main components: 'arms' and an enormous tetrapode base. These connect back to a single major concrete column which drop down into the retail area. The resulting pair of structural elements bring drama to the entrance of the events space.

above CAD axonometric view

right Physical model demonstrating the structural transfer

opposite Site construction photos

153

Mega Project: Logistic Endeavour

The transformation of the Power Station has required colossal feats of construction logistics creating unique adventures for the people involved. Although these feats may be invisible in the finished building, many have had an important impact on design decisions and leave their legacy.

Most construction activities have been carried out at a vast scale more typical of major infrastructure than a Grade II* Listed building. Every elevation inside and out had to be scaffolded and wrapped to its full height for the removal of asbestos before other construction work could even commence below. The height of these elevations required complex scaffolding, hoisting and lifting strategies just to reach the work faces. At one point there were 18 cranes on site which was momentarily more than in the whole City of London. As the new structural frame rose within the original walls, the permanent 72 lifts and escalators came into use. Vehicular movements on site had to be carefully managed with an anticipated frequency of one truck a minute at peak times. There is an endless list of uniquely complex activities spiralling to a daily spend of more than £1 million in construction cost at the busiest time.

The heritage significance and statutory protection were also key to the construction logistics. For example, the loss of original fabric associated with failed previous schemes had led to a planning condition to limit this risk by requiring each chimney be demolished and rebuilt in sequence rather than all together. Foundations had to be protected from new surrounding constructions with deep basements monitored continuously and all the retained structures were actively monitored throughout.

opposite Aerial view of Malaysia Square under construction

above 18 cranes on site

above left Malaysia Square paving installation

right Cranes inside the historic fabric

left Bridge suspended from historic gantry beam

below Scaffolding in Turbine Hall A during restoration of historic faience tiles

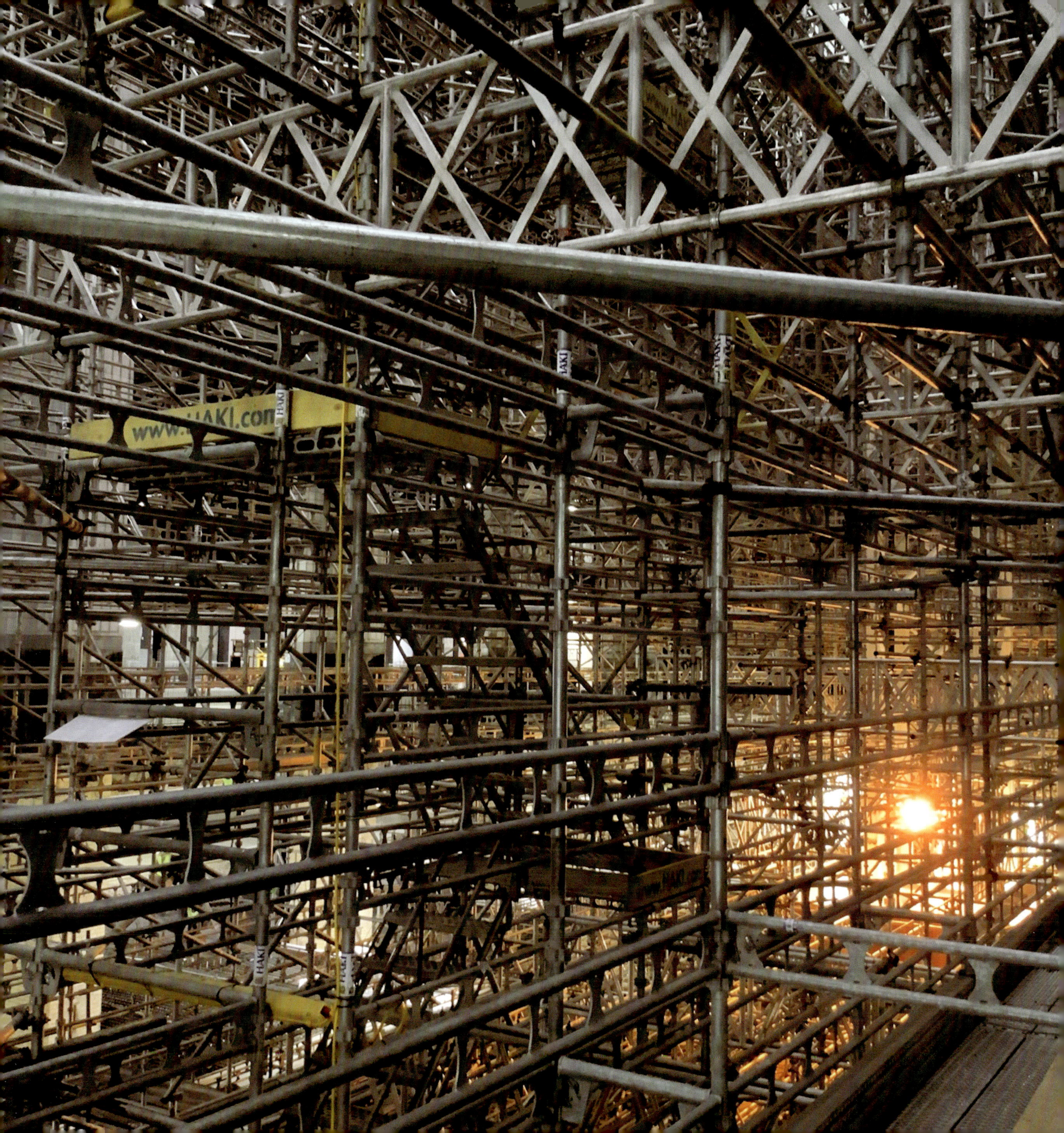
HAKI

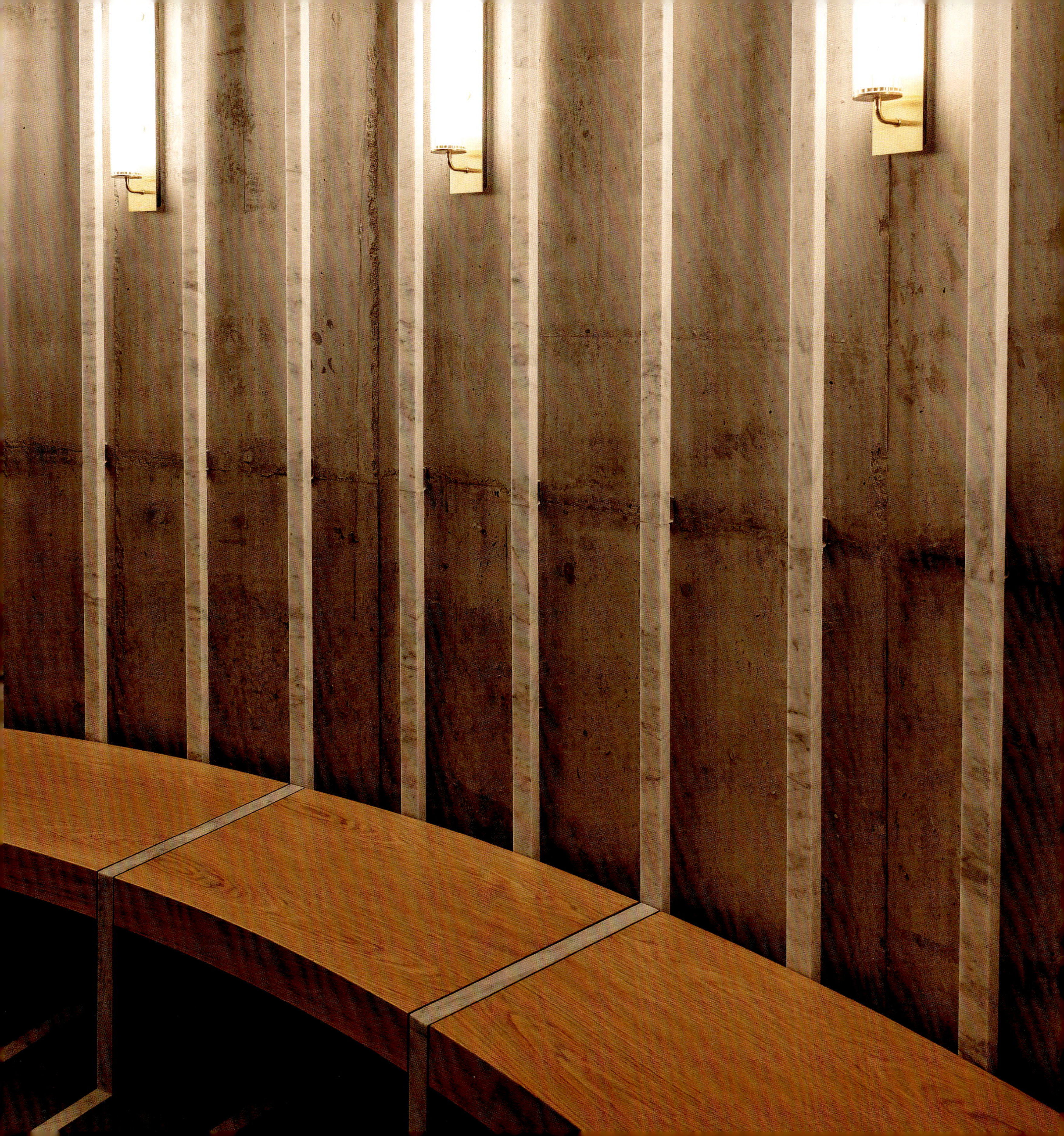

Drawings

6

Long Section, Cutting North-South

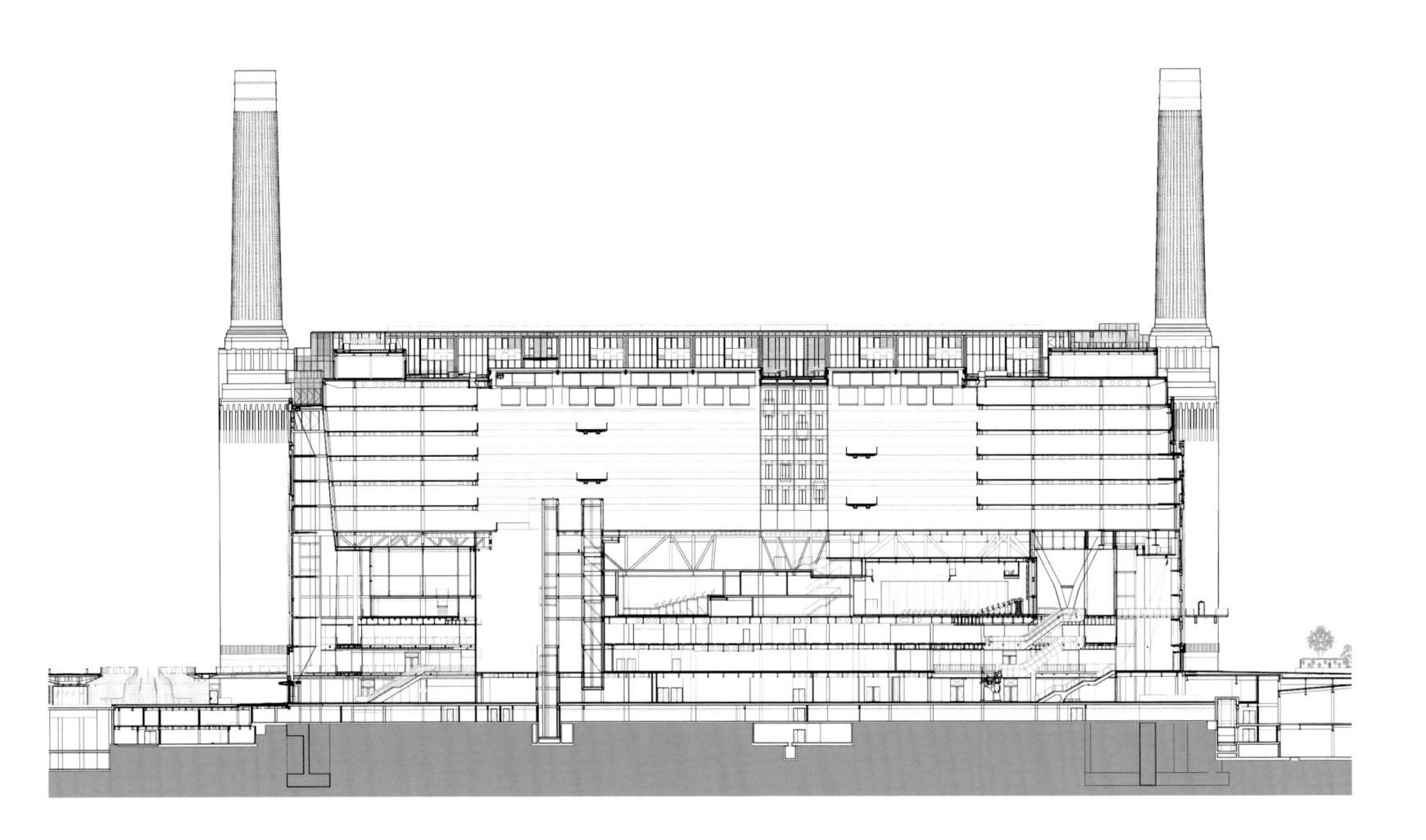

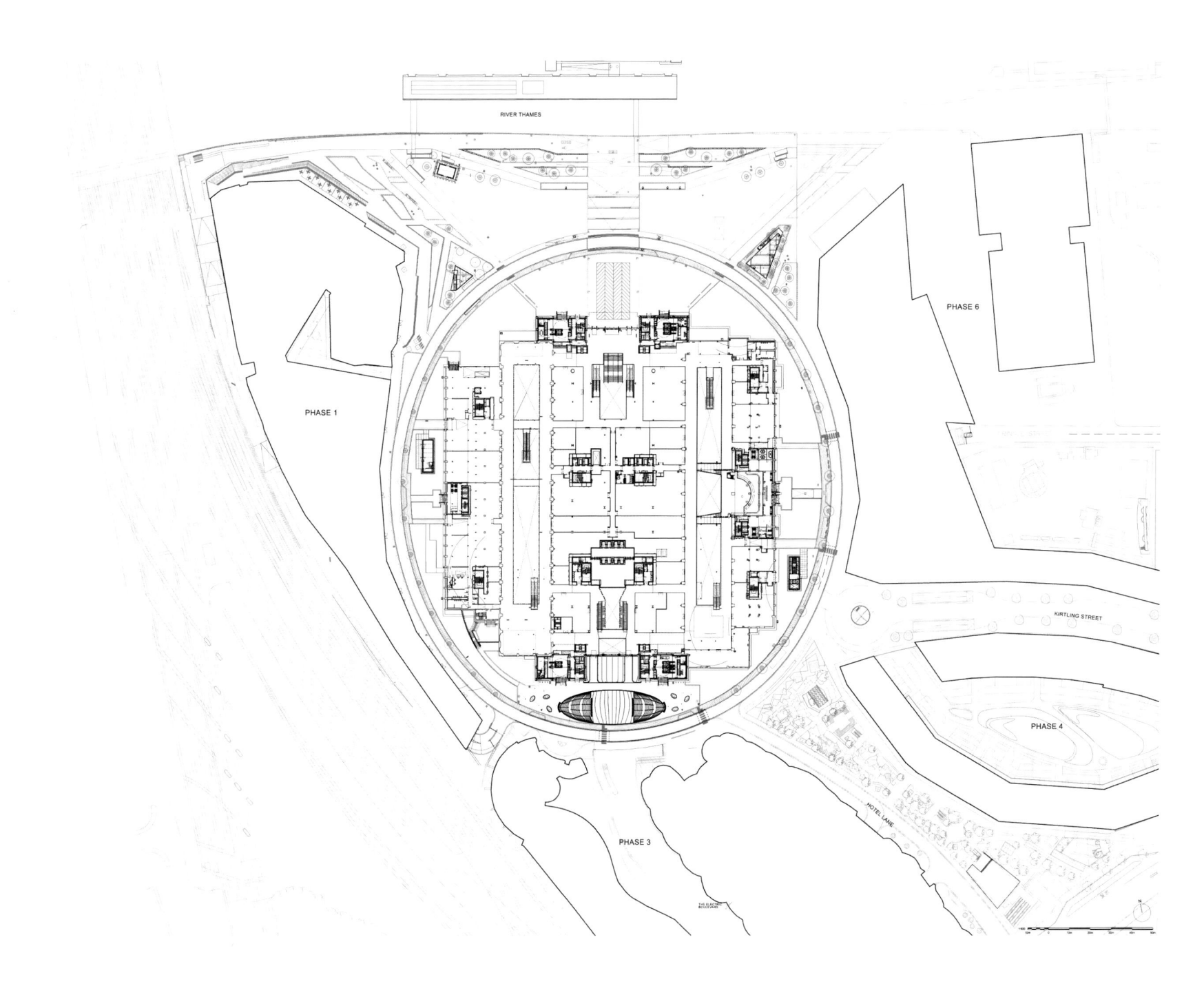

Site Plan

161

South Elevation

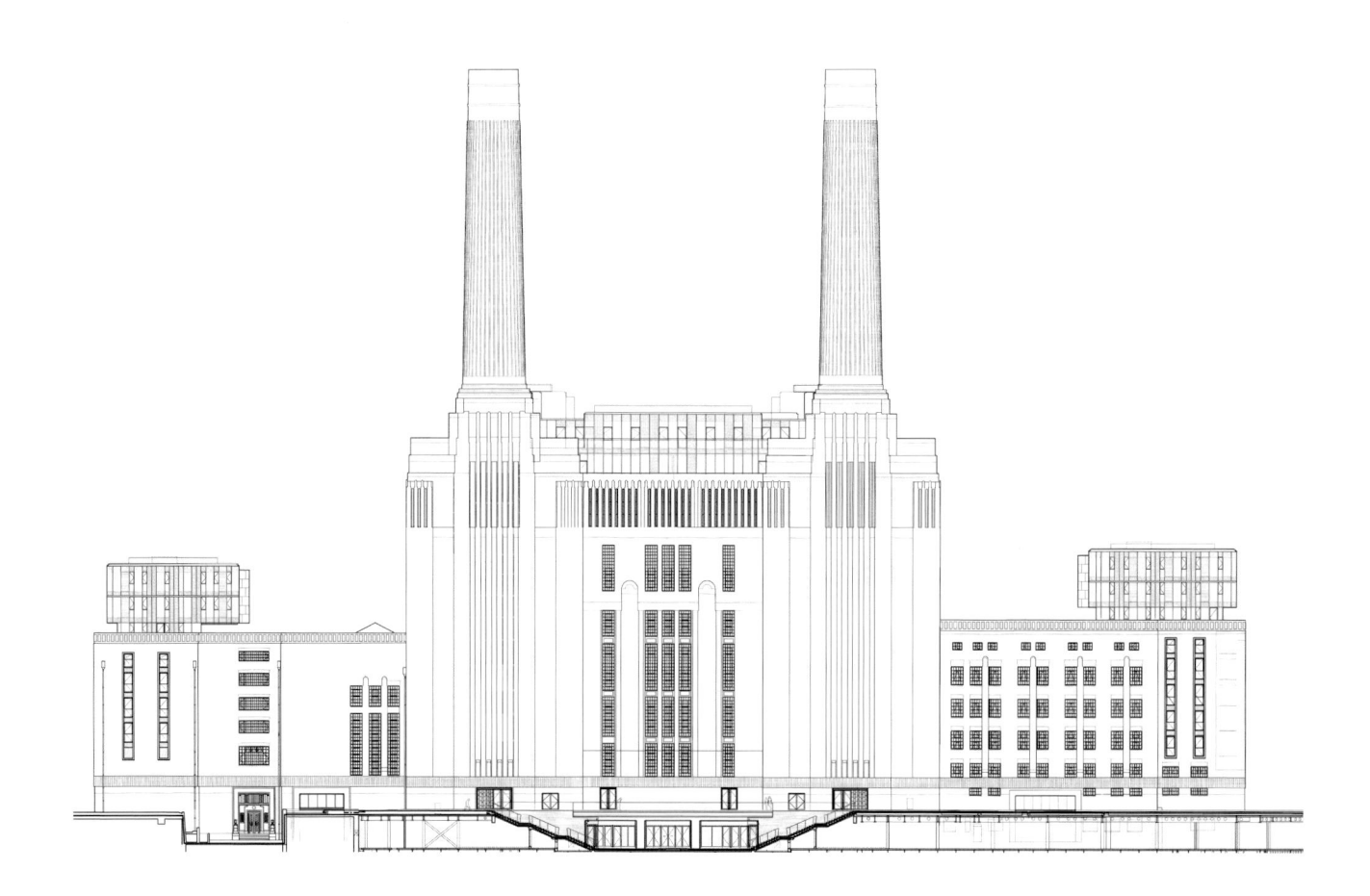

North Elevation

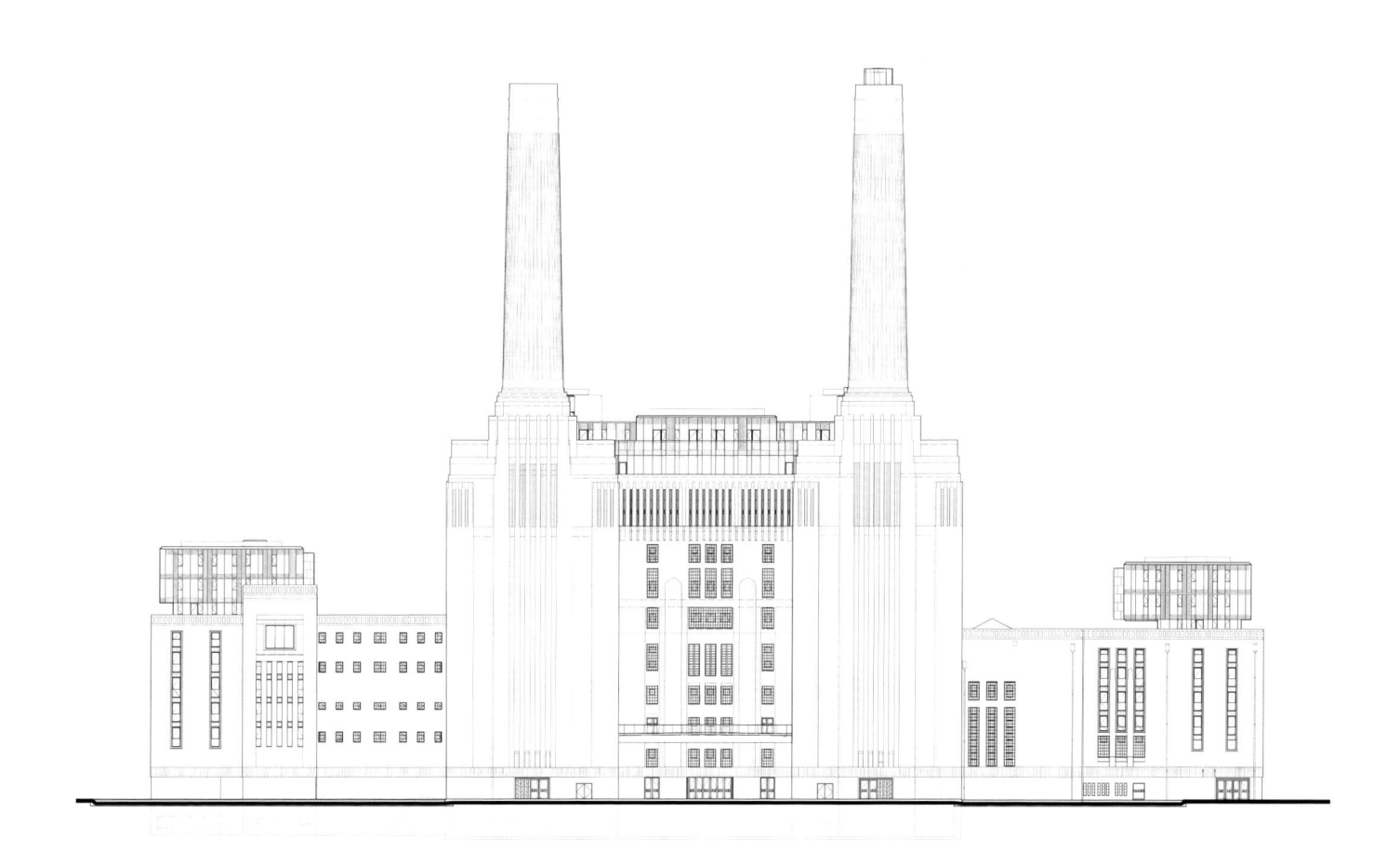

163

West Elevation

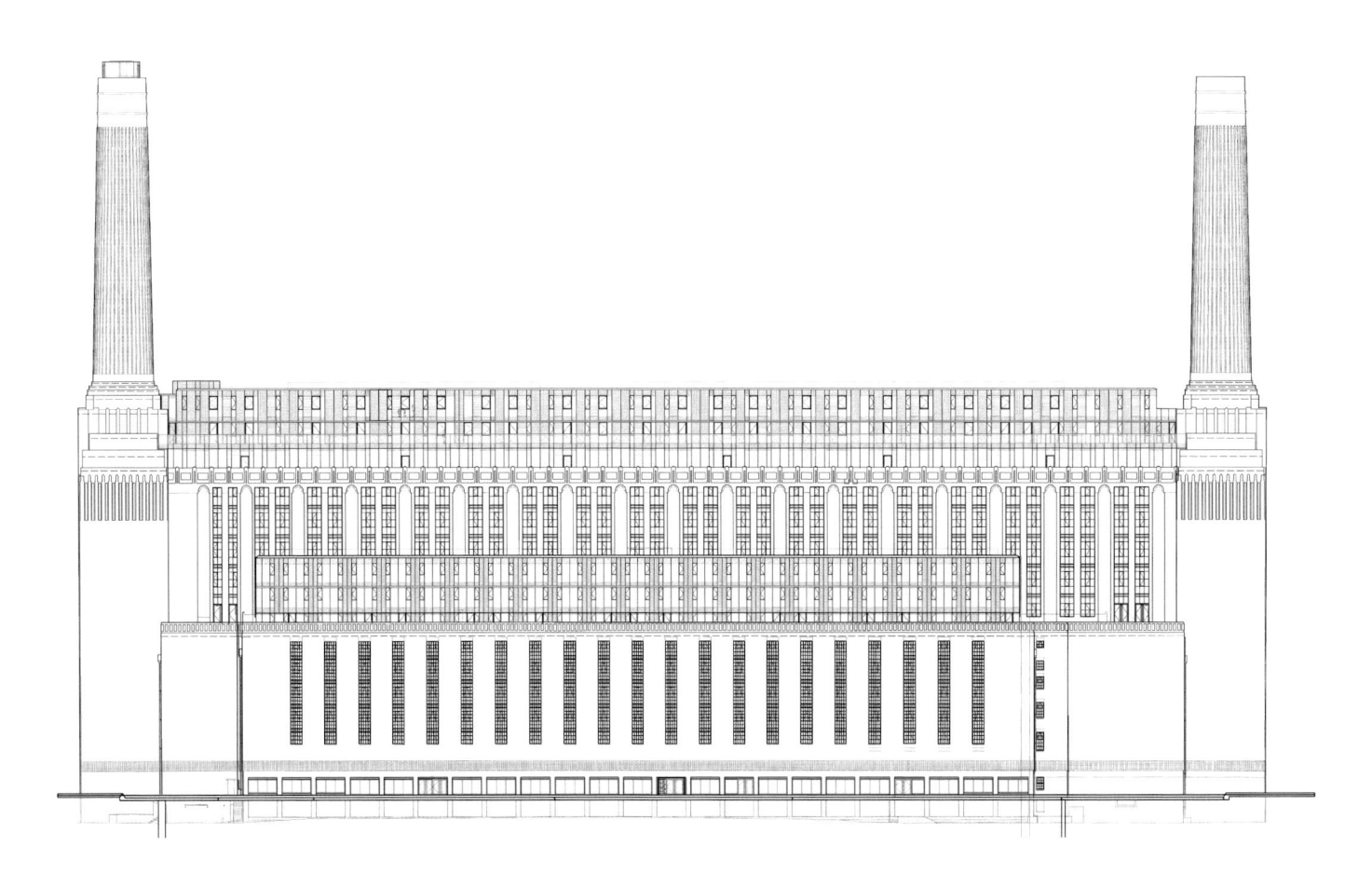

East Elevation

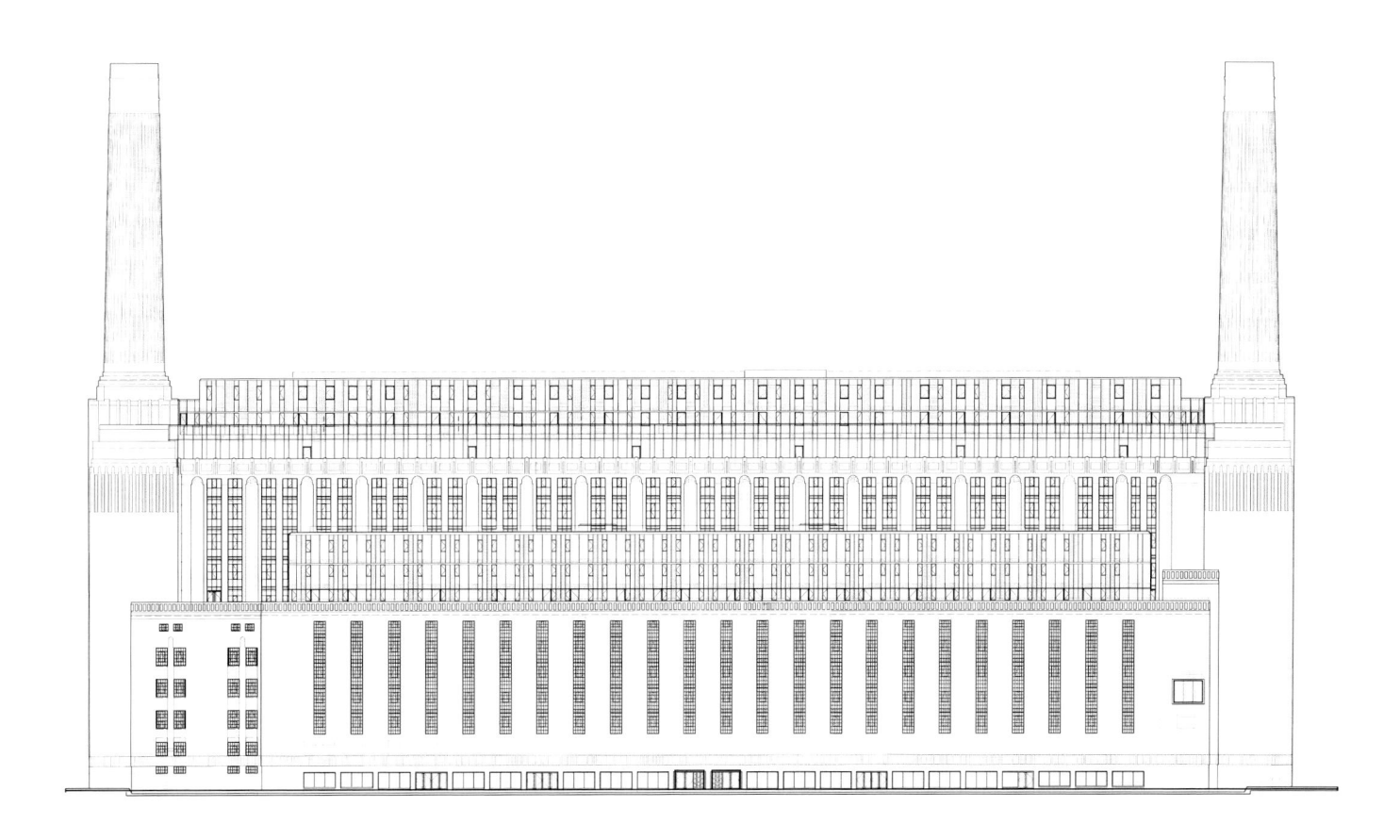

01 BANDSTAND UNDERSIDE OF DECK
1:25

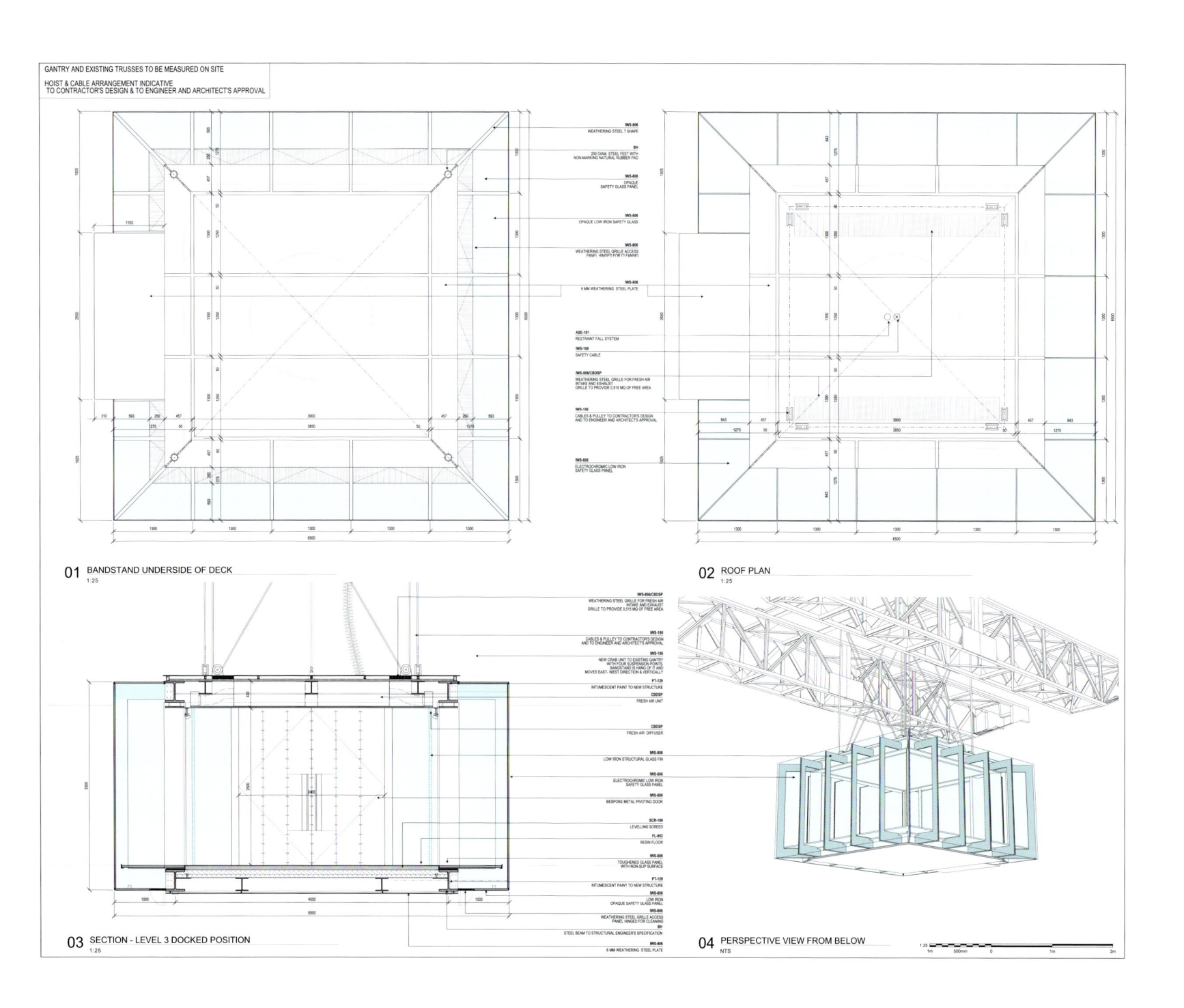

02 ROOF PLAN
1:25

03 SECTION - LEVEL 3 DOCKED POSITION
1:25

04 PERSPECTIVE VIEW FROM BELOW
NTS

Turbine Hall B Bandstand

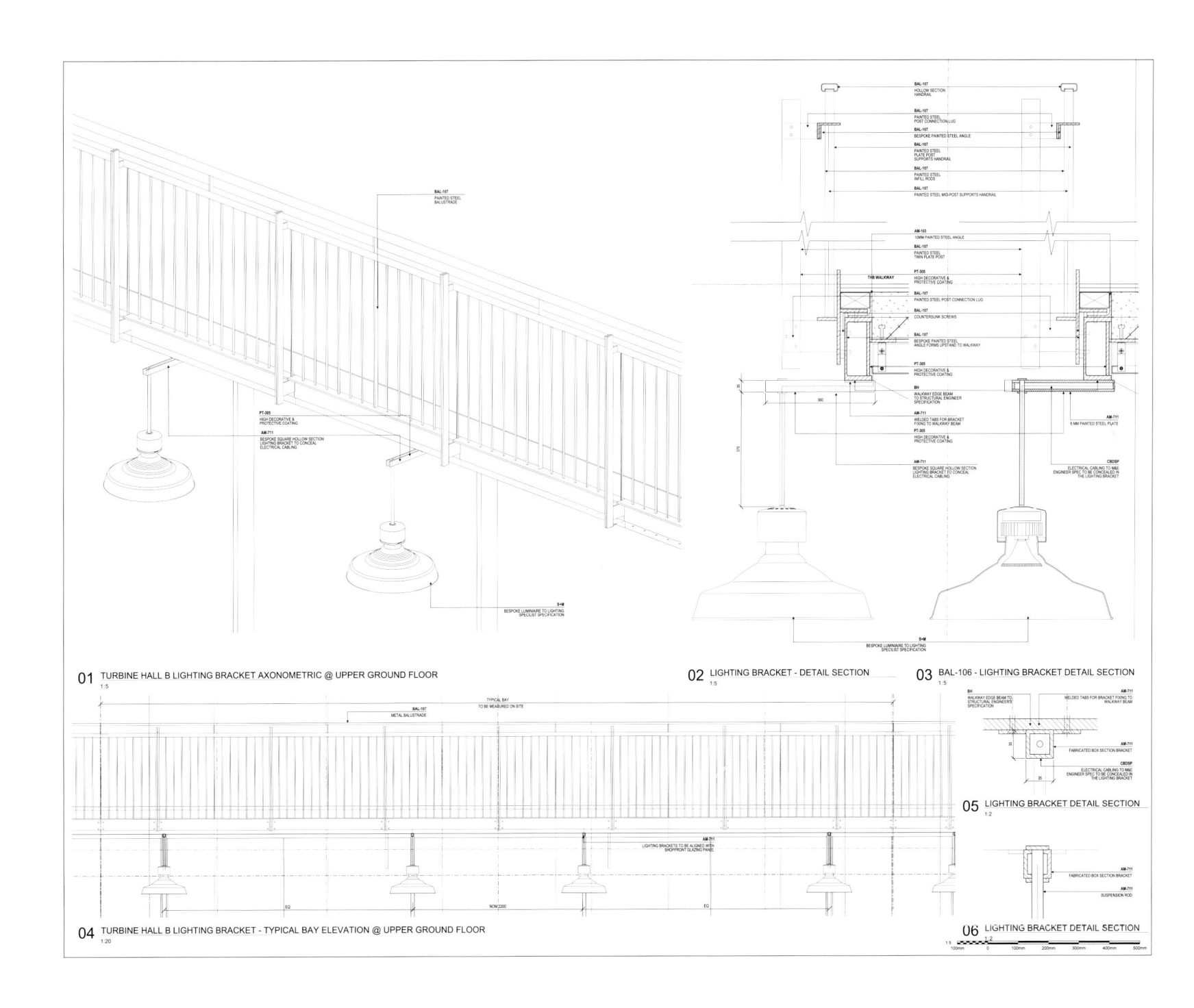

01 TURBINE HALL B LIGHTING BRACKET AXONOMETRIC @ UPPER GROUND FLOOR
1:5

02 LIGHTING BRACKET - DETAIL SECTION
1:5

03 BAL-106 - LIGHTING BRACKET DETAIL SECTION
1:5

04 TURBINE HALL B LIGHTING BRACKET - TYPICAL BAY ELEVATION @ UPPER GROUND FLOOR
1:20

05 LIGHTING BRACKET DETAIL SECTION
1:2

06 LIGHTING BRACKET DETAIL SECTION
1:2

Turbine Halls Balustrade Detail

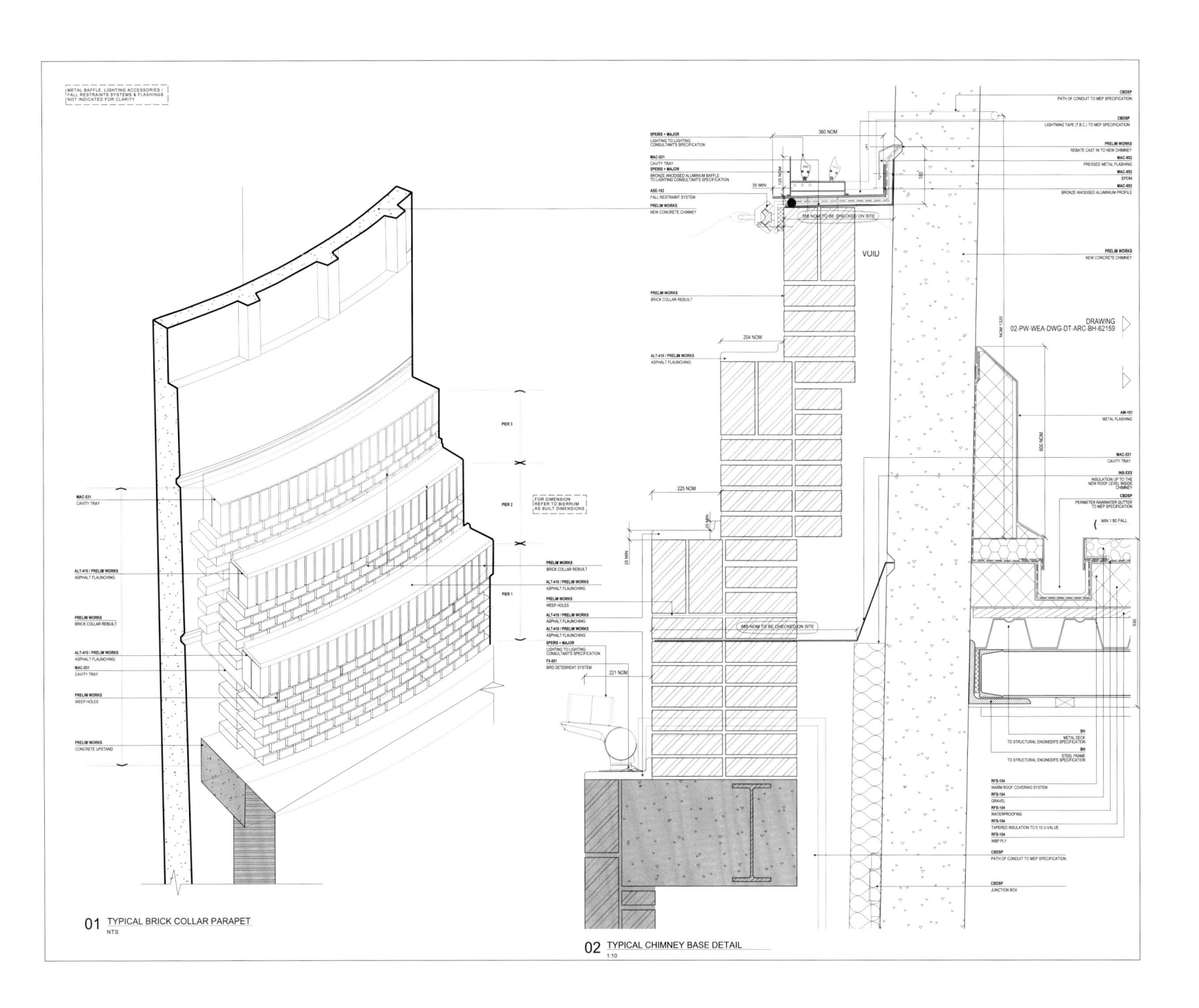

Wash Tower to Chimney Connection

01 CHIMNEY LIFT CAR - ISOMETRIC VIEW

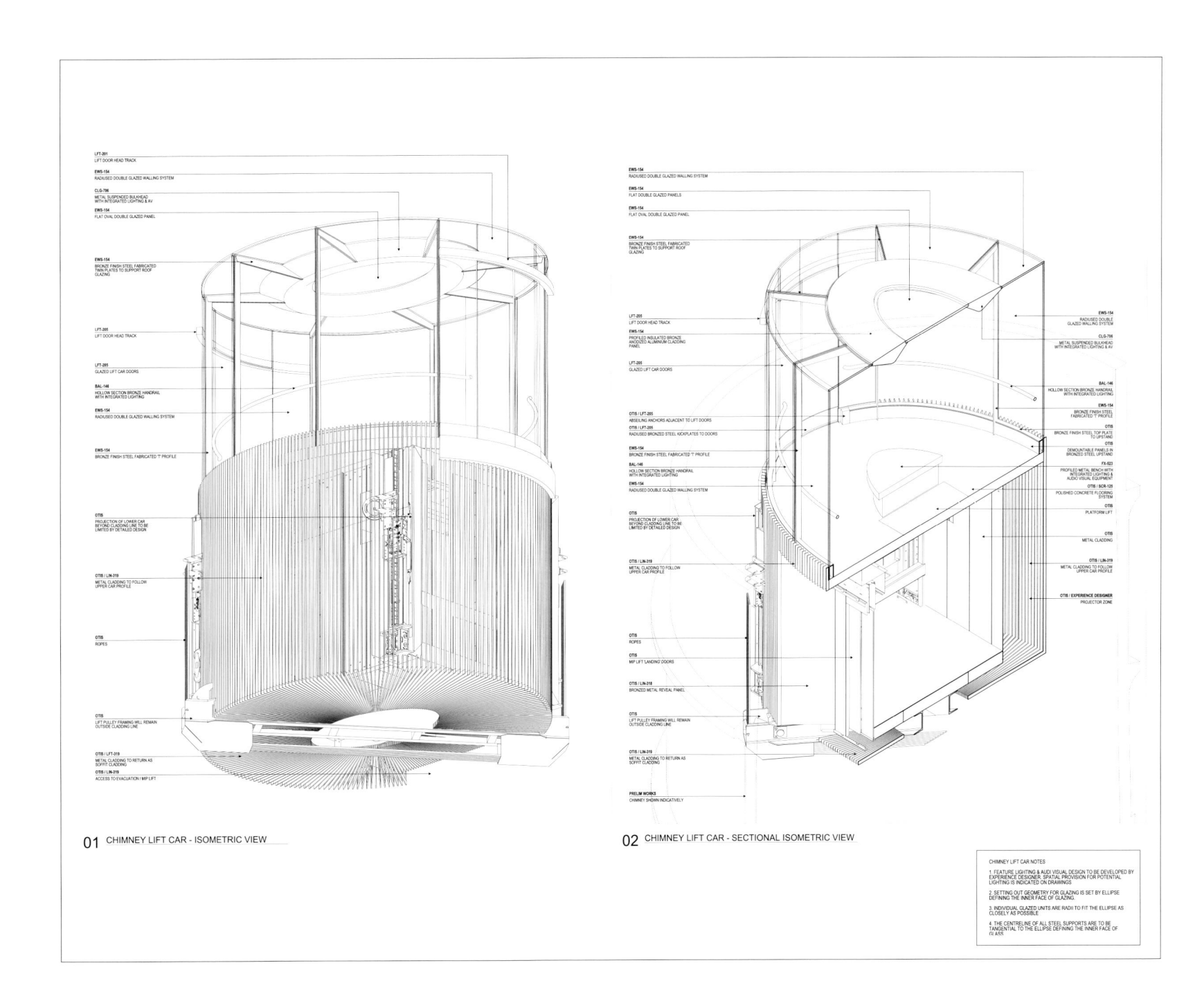

02 CHIMNEY LIFT CAR - SECTIONAL ISOMETRIC VIEW

CHIMNEY LIFT CAR NOTES

1. FEATURE LIGHTING & AUDIO VISUAL DESIGN TO BE DEVELOPED BY EXPERIENCE DESIGNER. SPATIAL PROVISION FOR POTENTIAL LIGHTING IS INDICATED ON DRAWINGS

2. SETTING OUT GEOMETRY FOR GLAZING IS SET BY ELLIPSE DEFINING THE INNER FACE OF GLAZING.

3. INDIVIDUAL GLAZED UNITS ARE RADII TO FIT THE ELLIPSE AS CLOSELY AS POSSIBLE

4. THE CENTRELINE OF ALL STEEL SUPPORTS ARE TO BE TANGENTIAL TO THE ELLIPSE DEFINING THE INNER FACE OF GLASS

Chimney Lift Car

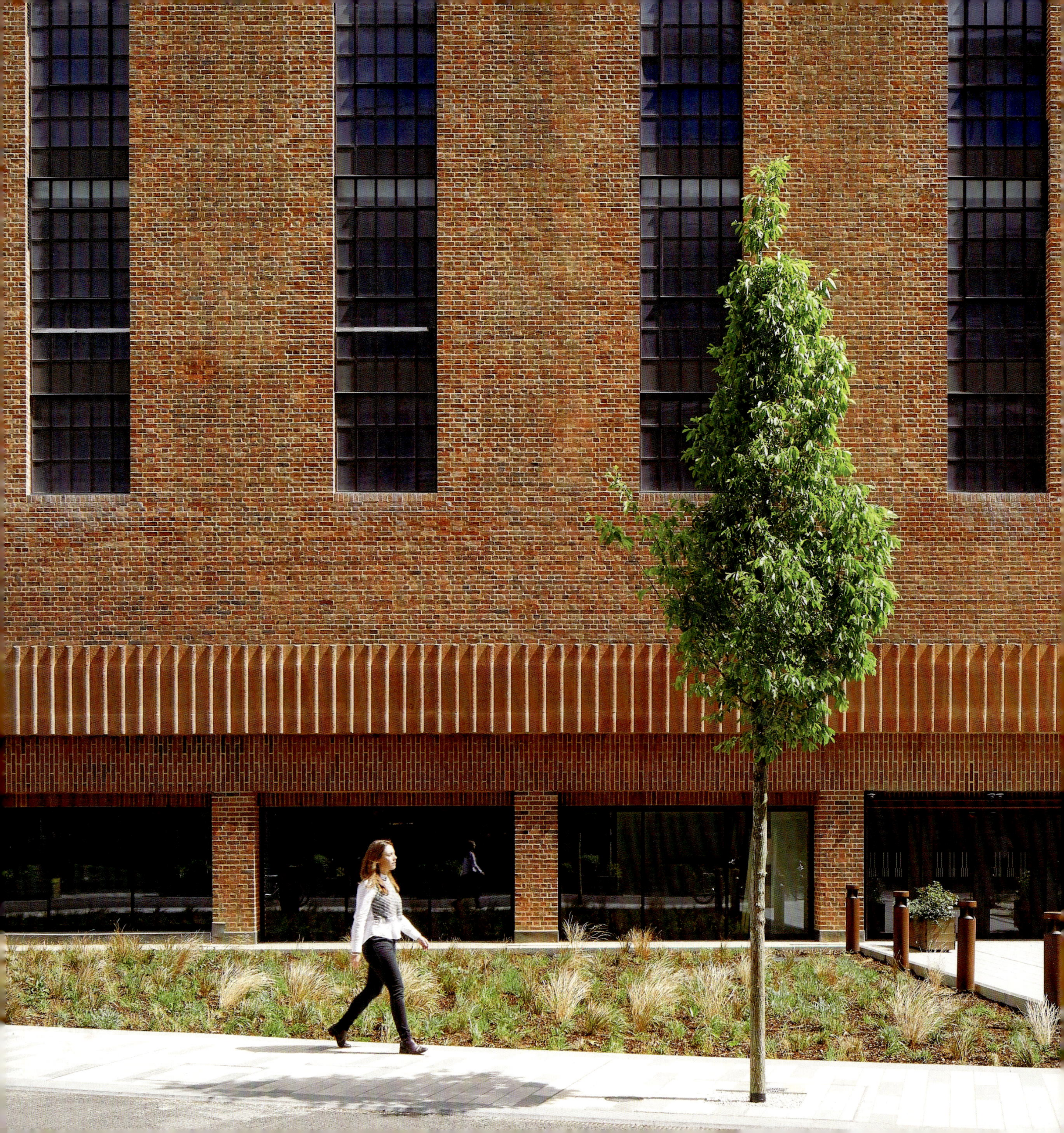

Building Legacy

Giving back to the Londoner

7

Giving Back to Londoners

The Power Station reopened its doors in October 2022, ending four decades of dilapidation and ushering in a new era for the building as the centre of a thriving London neighbourhood. Crucially, and unlike its previous enigmatic incarnation, the building is now open to the public and can be experienced by everyone. At the heart of a steadily unfolding masterplan, which includes a new tube station, Battersea Power Station is now a London destination - in its first year of opening alone, it welcomed more than 10 million visitors. The building has been so successful, in fact, that the area has been recategorised on London's Tube Map as Zone 1.

The turbine halls are frequented 24/7 by residents, locals and tourists alike, while the public spaces in its vicinity are host to both casual lunchbreaks and family daytrips to enjoy the colourful array of activities hosted by the Battersea Power Station Development Company. From fashion shows to an 'Olympic Race Track,' there is always something to capture the imagination, cementing the building into the Londoner's psyche as a creative, social and commercial hub.

173

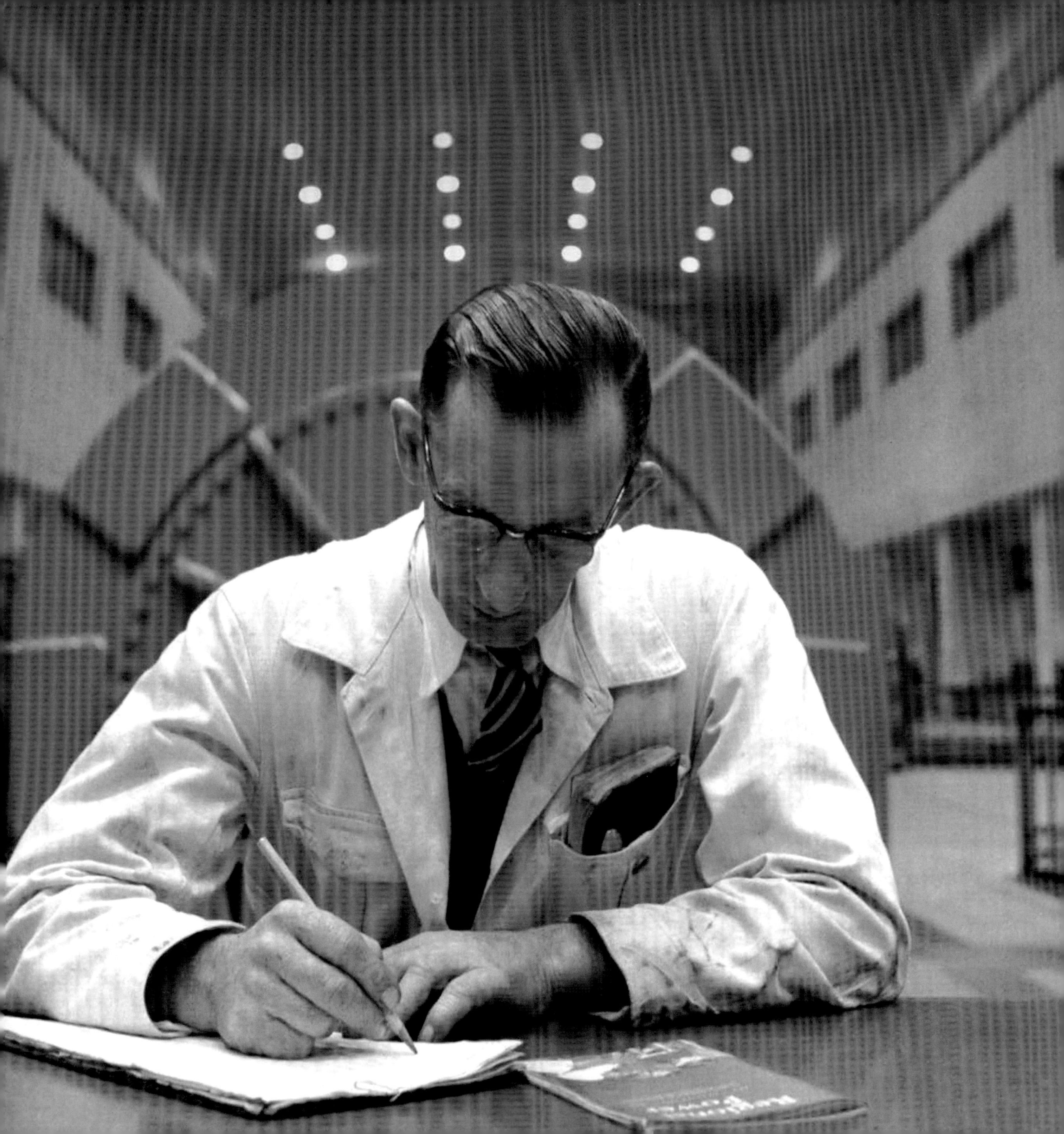

Acknowledgements
Design team and credits

8

Team Credits

Architect | WilkinsonEyre

Team from 2013 to 2022 in alphabetical order: Adam Justice, Adam Price, Alastair Speak, Aleca Haeger, Aleksandra Kravchenko, Aleksy Dojnow, Alessandro Filippi, Alexandra Neill, Anastasia Gravani, Anna Woodeson, Anneli Giencke, Andrea Wu, Andre Mariani, Andy Brisk, Anthony Crescini, Artemis Karaiskou, Atila Tasan, Babak Tizkar, Ben Bisek, Ben Carter, Cecilia Lubbock, Cely Bigando, Charlotte Harding, Chris Davies, Damien Ilev, Dan Cotton, David Oakes, Davide Agentiere, Dayo Oladunjoye, Dom Benzecry, Dominga Garufi, Dominik Langloh, Dominic Wilkinson, Ed Daines, Edward Couper, Ehab AlFaraj, Efthymia Kotsani, Eleni Pavlidou, Emma Kate Mathews, Emma Mooney, Emily James, Frédéric André, Gareth Kirkman, Gary Dupont, George Hintzen, Geoffrey Whittaker, Gunay Demirci, Hannah Lewis, Holly Neal, Helen Floate, Hyunjin Kim, Ivan Subanovic, Ivana Bocina, James Barrington, James Leung, James Llewellyn, Jason Cope, Javier Briasco, Javier Esquembre, James Smith, Jekatirina Kowaltschuk, Jemma Laird, Jess Hall, Jim Eyre, Jiwon Lee, Jose Llerena, Julian Caballero, Justin Frank, Justin Lau, Katherine Graham, Kathleen Laskin, Lara Yegenoglu, Laura Kovic, Lia Ronez, Luke Clayden, Luca Vernocchi, Lucian Mocanu, Marcello Licitra, Marco Corazza, Marco Pantaleoni, Mark Smith, Marta Lobasz, Marwan Abdo, Matthew Downey, Maxime Monin, Miya Ushida, Nicole Gaskin, Oscar McDonald, Peter Hinchliffe, Phoebe Eustance, Rebecca Granger, Rita Vekaria, Roberta Colombo, Robertson Ahomka-Lindsay, Ronghua Lei, Sam Wright, Sanjiv Sangha, Sarah Agill, Sebastien Ricard, Sean Shea, Sheryl Lam, Soo Yau, Sofia Nowak, Thomas Carpentier, Thomas Reeves, Thomas Murray, Thomas Penny, Tim Tasker, Valentina Miceli, Veronika Martykan, Vidhya Pushpanathan, Victor Nordheim, Vita Giannini, Vlad Dumitru, Xenia Cosmas, Yee Fei Tan

Client | Malaysian Investor Consortium

Comprising PNB, Sime Darby Property, S P Setia and the Employees' Provident Fund

Development Manager | Battersea Power Station Development Company (BPSDC)
Structural Engineer | Buro Happold
Mechanical Engineer | ChapmanBDSP MEP
Construction Manager | MACE
Lighting Designer | Speirs Major
Interior Apartment Designer | Michaelis Boyd
Project Manager | Turner & Townsend
Cost Consultant | Gardiner & Theobald
Planning Consultant | DP9
External Landscaping | LDA Design
Roof Garden Design | Andy Sturgeon
Conservation Consultant | Purcell
Facade Engineer | Buro Happold Façade
Fire Engineer | Buro Happold Fire
Transport Engineer | Steer
CDM Consultant | IM2 Ltd
Security Consultant | QCIC
Acoustic Consultants | Aecom acoustics, Neill Woodger Acoustic & Theatre Design
Signage Consultant | Holmes Woods
Facade Access Consultant | REEF
Accessibility Consultant | BHID

177

Image Credits

Ben Bisek *50*
Bridget Bishop *15, 174*
James Budgen *63, 88, 153, 158*
Brian Barnes/BPSCG *17*
Battersea Power Station Development Company *8, 33*
Hufton + Crow Photography *8, 22, 90, 95–103, 126, 127, 130, 136, 137, 147, 148, 170, 180*
Hulton Deutsch *6*
Farrells *20*
Alex Fedorenko *155*
Monty Fresco *8, 15*
Jason Hawkes *92, 124*
Peter Hinchliffe *144, 177*
Elodie Kowalski *75, 101*
Peter Landers *1, 62, 67, 69, 71, 74, 81, 88, 89, 109, 116, 128, 129, 139, 141, 145, 148, 173*
Andrew Lee *117, 118*
John Outram Architects *20*
Jim Stephenson *4, 57, 60, 61, 149*
John Sturrock *8, 58, 65, 66, 70, 125*
Rachel Warne/Andy Sturgeon *91*

Fox Photos/Getty *8, 12, 13, 14*
Daily Herald Archive/Getty *11*
PA Images/Alamy *8, 17*
Joseph Toth/Alamy *21*
European Sports Photo Agency/Alamy *21*

Special thanks from Sebastien Ricard

Many people have contributed to the success of the transformation of Battersea Power Station: architects, engineers, landscapers, contractors, advisors, local authorities, Historic England, the shareholders back in Malaysia and the client representatives based in UK. And indeed the many millions of people who have visited since the building opened to the public.

In helping to produce this book we are especially grateful to Emilie Lemons and John Booth and the help from the ORO's team.

Finally my biggest thanks go to the WilkinsonEyre's team without whom none of this would have been possible. Their hard work and generosity with their time for almost 10 years has been without match and they made this incredible adventure so much fun. A special thanks to James Llewelyn, Marwan Abdo, Chris Davies, Helen Floate, Ivan Subanovic, James Barrington, Marco Corazza and many others and Jim Eyre for his ideas, advice and insight.

WilkinsonEyre

ISBN 978-1-961856-85-1